THE
PHILOSOPHER
QUEENS

THE
PHILOSOPHER
QUEENS

The lives and legacies of philosophy's unsung women

Edited by

REBECCA BUXTON AND LISA WHITING

unbound

First published in 2020

Unbound

6th Floor Mutual House, 70 Conduit Street, London W1S 2GF

www.unbound.com

Illustrations © Emmy Smith

Text design by Patty Rennie

A CIP record for this book is available from the British Library

ISBN 978-1-78352-801-1 (trade)
ISBN 978-1-78352-829-5 (ebook)

Printed in Slovenia by DZS-Grafik

1 3 5 7 9 8 6 4 2

For our sisters

With special thanks to Carole Edmond
for generously supporting this book

Contents

Introduction

Most people don't think of Plato's *Republic* as a work of feminist philosophy. But when Plato proposed that women, as well as men, were capable of leading the ideal city-state, he was thinking far ahead of his time. Plato argued, through the voice of Socrates, that talented and intelligent women should be chosen to work alongside men as Guardians. These 'Philosopher Kings', as they are often called, would rule over the Republic, providing perfect philosophical enlightenment and bringing harmony to the city.

Over 2,000 years later, you would forgive people for assuming that men have been doing most of the philosophy since then. Women do not seem to have fulfilled Plato's prediction that they too could become great thinkers. Or, at least, that's how today's philosophy books make it look.

The history of philosophy has not done women justice. To see this, you only have to look at some of the recent books published on the topic. In *Philosophy: 100 Essential Thinkers* only two women feature, with Mary Wollstonecraft and Simone de Beauvoir taking the seats of honour. In *The Great Philosophers: From Socrates to Turing*, no women made the cut. Each chapter in that particular book was written by a contemporary philosopher, all of whom are also men. At the time of writing, a newly published book by A. C. Grayling, boldly titled *The History of Philosophy*, includes no sections on women philosophers. The book does include a three-and-a-half-page review of 'Feminist Philosophy' in which only one woman philosopher – Martha Nussbaum – is mentioned by name. You're beginning to sense a theme.

It's important to note that this gap is not due to a lack of books being published about philosophy generally. On the contrary, accessible texts are being written on an incredibly broad range of topics, such as *Golf and Philosophy: Lessons from the Links*, *Aristotle and an Aardvark Go to Washington*, and last but certainly not least, *Surfing with Sartre*. And yet, very little has been written to celebrate the work of great women philosophers. One notable exception was written by a great philosopher herself, Baroness Mary Warnock, who wrote *Women Philosophers* over twenty years ago.

It is of course true that women have been under-represented in philosophy, and indeed most of academia, because they were historically excluded from education. The first four women in the UK to receive degrees in any subject graduated in 1880 from University College London. The University of Cambridge was the last British institution to allow women to take full degrees, in 1948. This institutional exclusion meant that women were pre-scribed roles in society that kept their thinking, and their freedom, to a minimum.

But this is 2019 and things have certainly improved over the past century. More women are taking degrees in philosophy than ever before, with most universities now seeing higher numbers of women than men in their undergraduate classes. In spite of this progress, there is still a huge gender disparity higher up in the pecking order. There are very few philosophy departments where women make up anywhere near 50 per cent of faculty staff. In

2015, women accounted for only 22 per cent of philosophy professors at the twenty top US universities. In some fields of philosophy, there has been almost no increase in the number of women since the 1970s. So, even though more young women are taking their first dive into the man's world of philosophy than ever before, this is not quickly translating into more at the top. Where some women have secured lectureships and professorships, an overwhelming number of them are white. Non-white women are still hugely under-represented in philosophy, with very few senior positions filled by people from minority backgrounds. In her *New York Times* interview, 'The Pain and Promise of Black Women in Philosophy', Professor Anita L. Allen noted that only 1 per cent of full-time philosophy professors in the US are Black, whilst around 17 per cent are women.

When the two of us were studying philosophy at university, we knew that women were under-represented in our discipline. Both of us had only a handful of women lecturers, and our lessons were dominated by men from hundreds of years ago, as well as the men standing before us. A typical philosophy syllabus will likely feature very few or no women, with the focus instead being on the 'philosophical canon'. That is: Plato, Aristotle, Descartes, Hobbes, Locke, Hume, Rousseau, Kant, Mill, Nietzsche, Sartre and Rawls, to name only a few. Women are often only mentioned briefly, perhaps in reference to a male counterpart with whom they worked or had a relationship, or (if you're lucky) as part of a single 'Women in Philosophy' module. When attempts are made to diversify the curriculum to include other important philosophical voices, this is often accompanied by a media outcry over 'snowflake' students and lecturers.

Despite these frustrations, there is much cause for hope. Outstanding work is being done in academic philosophy to reclaim the history of women philosophers and ensure that their voices and perspectives are preserved for the next generation of thinkers. The New Narratives in the History of Philosophy group and Project Vox both showcase the work of women philosophers from the early modern period, 1500–1800. The Society for Women in Philosophy (SWIP) runs events and mentoring programmes aimed at promoting women in philosophy, past, present, and future. The Centre for the History of Women Philosophers and Scientists at Paderborn University, Germany, runs an annual summer school, teaching students about the great contribution that women have made to the history of thought. The In Parenthesis project at Durham University explores and archives the work of the Oxford four: Mary Midgley, Iris Murdoch, Elizabeth Anscombe and Philippa Foot. This year has also seen the publication of *Becoming Beauvoir* by one of our own authors, Kate Kirkpatrick. All of this work is helping to break down barriers for women in philosophy today, by showing that women in this field are far from new. We have, in fact, been philosophers all along.

There is still a long way to go to change popular perceptions of philosophy. When creating our promotional video for this book, we asked members of the public to name as many philosophers as they could. When they all listed the usual suspects, we asked whether they could name any *women* philosophers. None of the people that we surveyed could name a single one.

This book is an attempt to change these perceptions. In the pages that follow, we intentionally adopt a broad definition of 'philosopher' as we believe that part of the reason why women have historically been excluded from our discipline is because many of them have instead been considered activists or 'learned ladies'. This has led to a prevailing image of the white male philosopher thinking from his armchair. Instead, it's time to recognise the clear intellectual rigour, questioning and insight that makes these women worthy of the 'philosopher' title.

The authors and subjects in this book come from many different backgrounds with their own unique ideas, experiences and histories. The philosophers written about here are complex, challenging, often inspiring, and sometimes deeply problematic. However, they all contribute an important element to our understanding of philosophy. Some of them you will have heard of, or perhaps studied. Others you might encounter here for the first time. You can enjoy this book by simply selecting chapters that pique your interest or following along chronologically; the choice is yours. There have, of course, been many women whom we have not been able to include. You can find a list of other women philosophers in the More Philosopher Queens section at the back of the book. We encourage you to explore their lives and work for yourself.

So if you're interested in women and their ideas, this book will help you to learn about the many Philosopher Queens who have contributed to our world's rich intellectual history. We hope you enjoy getting to know these women as much as we have.

Rebecca & Lisa
LONDON, 2019

Diotima

c. 400 BCE

Zoi Aliozi

It may come as a surprise to some that Plato, often regarded as the founding father of philosophy, included a woman as a key character in one of his dialogues. His discussions with Diotima of Mantinea on the nature of love and beauty are immortalised in one of Plato's famous works, the *Symposium*. However, Diotima herself remains a mystery, with many arguing that she never existed at all. This difficult puzzle has shrouded much of Diotima's possible contribution to the history of ideas, which has not yet been fully appreciated or understood. Her teachings, if indeed they are hers, remain valuable 2,000 years on.

Diotima was one of the few women to feature in Plato's dialogues. Another was Aspasia of Miletus, who features in the *Menexenus*. Neither Diotima nor Aspasia appear as speakers in their own right in these dialogues. Instead Socrates recounts his previous arguments with them to his male interlocutors. Plato is also believed to have had women as students, most notably Axiothea of Phlius and Lastheneia of Mantinea.

Given her potential influence on such a key figure in the philosophical canon, we might wonder why Diotima has been somewhat ignored by academics, resembling more myth than historical figure. Some argue that Diotima was created by Plato as a literary device to exemplify what it means to be a good philosopher. This is thought to have been a method of adapting his argumentative style to his main discussant in the *Symposium*, Agathon. As Socrates notes in the *Phaedrus*, to have the power of speech one must know how to lead the soul, and to do so successfully, one must know the soul of one's interlocutor. Having a woman as his partner in argumentation might have been a way to make his position more persuasive.

Scholars, such as Mary Ellen Waithe in *A History of Women Philosophers* (1987), have begun to recognise Diotima as a historical figure. There are a few reasons why we might share this view. It is true that there is no definitive proof that a Greek philosopher named Diotima visited Athens, met with Socrates and taught him philosophy. We do know, however, that many of the characters in Plato's dialogues were real people, which perhaps makes Diotima's existence more likely. Some also believe that Socrates potentially sought out the opinions of other women, as he references receiving advice from wise men and women in *Meno*. That he would have spoken to a woman like Diotima on the nature of love is perhaps not so unlikely. We might further wonder whether claims that she was fictional stem from the disbelief that a woman of such intellect might have existed in Ancient Greece at all.

Even if Diotima was imagined by Plato, she is still worth recognising as an important woman in the history of philosophy. Fictional or not, her voice had a powerful influence on the arguments made by Socrates and therefore the history of philosophy as we know it. So, whether Diotima existed is not our main worry here. Let's simply acknowledge for the time being that our first Philosopher Queen is something of an enigma.

As we've noted, the character of Diotima plays an important role in Plato's dialogue, the *Symposium*, which contains all that we know about the philosophy attributed to her. A symposium was a gathering of men discussing various philosophical topics, usually following a banquet and drinks. In Plato's *Symposium*, though, there was one fundamental difference: there was a woman whose ideas enjoyed equal status with the male thinkers presented in the text. The protagonists in the *Symposium* are asked by their host, Agathon, to give speeches on the meaning of love. After listening to his companion's arguments, Socrates states that he was educated in 'the philosophy of love' by Diotima of Mantinea, describing her as a wise woman, philosopher and priestess. When introducing Diotima, Socrates also claims that she foresaw and successfully postponed the Plague of Athens by instructing the citizens to perform sacrifices and rituals; the figure of Diotima is therefore often associated with prophecy and foresight. Socrates used this as evidence of her intellectual superiority and, some argue, to contrast her higher knowledge with the earthly wisdom of the others who were present. Socrates recalls learning from Diotima's great wisdom. He claims that she engaged his younger self in what has become known as the Socratic method, an argumentative conversation involving an individual being asked a series of questions about their view or definition and being potentially led to an alternative position. The implication being that Diotima perhaps taught Socrates one of his greatest contributions to philosophy: his methodology.

Socrates goes on to discuss his meetings with Diotima as a young student. Here, he outlines her teachings on the theory of Beauty and presents Diotima's ladder or 'the ladder of love', for which this dialogue is best known. Diotima's ladder places desire and lust for one attractive body at the bottom of the ladder, and this can lead towards an appreciation of the Form of Beauty, the highest point of the ladder. There are six steps on the ladder of love. First, the love of one individual body. Second, the love of all beautiful bodies. Third, the love of the beauty that a soul can have. Fourth, a love for beautiful public institutions, and then fifth, a love for knowledge in general. Finally, the lover will develop love for Beauty itself, which Diotima describes as 'looking upon a vast sea of Beauty'. The appreciation of Beauty itself brings with it the moral characteristic of virtue. She goes on to say that he who develops a love for Beauty itself 'will create many fair and noble thoughts and notions in boundless love of wisdom; until on that shore he grows and waxes strong, and at last the vision is revealed to him of a single science, which is the science of beauty everywhere'. An appreciation of Beauty therefore requires moving beyond appearances and instead learning to comprehend the abstract Idea of Beauty.

This discussion is closely related to Plato's famous theory of The Forms. Throughout many of his dialogues, Plato argued that Ideas or Forms are the non-physical essence of things in the changing, physical world. Plato therefore believed that we could not have knowledge of objects in the physical world because they are merely imitations of the eternal realm of the Forms. In order to achieve knowledge, as opposed to merely opinions, one must turn away from the world of perceptions and shadows and towards the world of Ideas, the most important of which was The Form of the Good. It's not clear whether the Good is a Form in the same way as other Forms, like Beauty or Justice. The Form of the Good, Plato tells us in the *Republic*, is instead 'beyond Being' and 'makes all things intelligible'. The best-known illustration of this is Plato's allegory of the cave.

However, it is not obvious that Diotima's concept of the Good or the Beautiful is the same as Plato's. Diotima argues that Beauty is not the end but the means to something greater. It is the achievement of a type of reproduction and the path towards immortality. Diotima explains this through her discussion of pregnancy. When Socrates asks Diotima, 'What is the function of love?' she responds, 'It is a childbirth in something beautiful, both in respect of body and of soul.' When Socrates says he does not understand, Diotima replies, 'All human beings are pregnant, Socrates, in body and in soul, and when we reach maturity it is natural that we desire to give birth.' We should note that Diotima is not always referring to pregnancy in the conventional sense. Instead, she often talks about pregnancy as part of the reproduction of ideas as well as of human beings. Those pregnant in the body seek a partner with whom to have children and create an heir. Those pregnant in the mind instead seek people with whom they can share their knowledge and virtue. Diotima continues, 'Who, when he thinks of Homer and Hesiod and other great poets, would not rather have their children than ordinary human ones? Who would not emulate them in the creation of children such as theirs, which have preserved their memory and given them everlasting glory?' The ultimate form of immortality is achieved through sharing and giving ideas to others, therefore creating intellectual offspring, as Homer and Hesiod have done. This form of reproduction, Diotima believed, was the function of Beauty. As Mary Ellen Waithe puts it, 'For Diotima the Good is a selfish good; one's own good is the acquisition of immortality by reproducing oneself through the idea of the Beautiful.' The Good therefore does not appear to function.

So, what should we learn from the mystery of Diotima of Mantinea? When discussing her ideas, Socrates recognises his own ignorance, and his willingness to learn from her obvious wisdom. During her discussion with Socrates she says with confidence, 'Of course I'm right!' and emphasises his inability to keep up with her argument. When Socrates asks, 'Most wise Diotima, is what you say really true?' he recalls, 'Like the accomplished sophists, she said, "You can be sure of that, Socrates."' That such a powerful woman was potentially present at such an important time in the history of philosophy should act as a call to women philosophers everywhere. Whether she was fictional or not, the ideas attributed to her matter, and we should do our best to channel the confidence and intellect of Diotima. Even when arguing with one of the founding fathers of philosophy.

Ban Zhao

45–120 CE

Eva Kit Wah Man

Ban Zhao is perhaps the greatest intellectual woman in ancient Chinese history. Together with sixteen other women, Ban's brief biography appears as 'the wife of Cao Shishu' in the collection 'Biographies of Exemplary Women' in the *Book of the Later Han*. Born in the early years of the Eastern Han dynasty (25–220 CE), she was the daughter of the well-known writer and historian Ban Biao (3–54 CE) and the younger sister of the general and diplomat Ban Chao (32–102 CE) and historian Ban Gu (32–92 CE). She was married at the age of fourteen to Cao Shishu. When her husband died young, Ban refused to remarry in observance of the tradition of widowhood that honours the virtue of chastity. Therefore, Ban conducted herself totally in keeping with her status and in conformity with the rules and standards of the time.

The most outstanding achievement of Ban's dazzling career was her contribution to the *Book of Han*, a history covering the twelve emperors from Emperor Gaozu to Emperor Ping, whose reigns spanned 300 years of the Western Han dynasty, which preceded the Eastern Han dynasty. The *Book of Han* was originally started by Ban's father Ban Biao and continued by her brother Ban Gu, who died before finishing the script. Known as 'broadly learned and superior in her talent', Ban was ordered by the Emperor He of the Eastern Han dynasty to complete the book. At the same time she was summoned to the palace to give instructions in proper conduct to the empress and the imperial concubines. She wrote narrative poems, commemorations, inscriptions, eulogies, arguments, commentaries, elegies, essays and other works until she died in her old age.

Ban earned her unique place in ancient Chinese history, not only for her learning on what constituted ideal womanhood and her writings intended to educate upper-class women, but also for her chastity, which had a great historical and philosophical impact. In general, she has been regarded as a pioneer of women's education and a paragon to be emulated by Chinese women. Her texts, for example *Lessons for Women* and 'Rhapsody on an Eastward Journey', and the treatises inspired by her life, were well received by Chinese, Korean and Japanese orthodox scholars, especially during the later Qing dynasty.

However, when the West met the East and the East became a subject of Western study in the twentieth century, the views of the orthodox scholars, who praised her as a pioneer of women's education, began to evolve and Ban's significance was re-evaluated. For example, Ban was described as an enemy of the cause of women by the women's liberation movement during the late Qing and early Republican era. A much more neutral stand sees Ban as neither heroine nor villain, but a faithful recorder of conventional views regarding relations between the sexes and appropriate behaviour for women. These points of view, along with the praise by earlier scholars, reflect a current heightened interest in Chinese gender studies in general.

Lessons for Women is unquestionably Ban's most important and influential work. As the first completed text devoted to women's learning compiled by Ban, it was likely written in 106 CE, when Ban was sixty-one years old. The text is given in the biography of Ban in the *Book of the Later Han*. It consists of seven short chapters, covering seven topics: humility, husband and wife, respect and caution, womanly qualities, wholehearted devotion, implicit obedience, and harmony with younger brothers and sisters-in-law. The text discusses how women establish their proper relation to others in the family and keep their honour and reputation in society. In the brief introduction, Ban first expresses her gratitude to her scholarly father and cultured mother for the education and training she received. Her education, she states, enabled her to successfully escape her fear of disgracing her parents or creating difficulties for her husband's relatives. After claiming that she no longer has any concerns for her son, as he has grown up and successfully entered an official career, Ban writes that her only remaining anxiety is for her daughters (not necessarily only Ban's own daughters, but also the girls of her family), who are of marrying age. Thus, Ban's intent in composing these seven chapters of instructions was to provide her daughters with guidance for achieving domestic harmony and for leading a better life once they entered into the hostile environment of their husbands' families. It was assumed disrespect, accusations, quarrels and overt confrontation were inevitable, particularly if the wife could not remain in her proper place, namely complete submission.

The relationship between husband and wife is the most important topic in *Lessons for Women*. *Yin* and *yang*, as the ultimate principles of Heaven and Earth, are the basis for how the relationship between husband and wife is defined. A man represents *yang*, the quality of which is rigidity, honoured by his strength. A woman represents *yin*, the function of which is yielding, appreciated due to her gentleness. The natural order of the interaction between *yin* and *yang* is essentially that *yang* controls the *yin* and *yin* serves the *yang*, which legitimises the conjugal ethics of women controlled by men and men served by women.

However, when we focus on the moral teachings of how a wife should serve her husband and classify Ban's precepts as Confucian womanly virtues, we might overlook the complicated relationships in the family life or oversimplify the interaction between the sexes as mere controlling of women by men, especially if we keep in mind the analogy of *yin* and *yang*. For Ban, the most important principles for a wife's conduct are respect and acquiescence. Although Ban adopts many keywords traditionally associated with femininity when she elaborates on the principles with instructions – for example, terms such as weakness, softness, inferiority, malleability – it is interesting to see how she actually describes the practical reasons for abiding by the principles. She determines, for example, that the heart of disrespect originates from the habit of the two spouses staying too close to one another. She also says that accusations and quarrels in family affairs are derived from bluntness and crookedness in words. Here, respect and acquiescence are recommended as a result of what Ban observed in married life in reality, not because of some moral and ethical deduction.

This suggests an alternative explanation, corresponding to Ban's own statement in the introduction to the text that her intention is to provide young wives with a survival kit necessary for marriage. In this sense, it is interesting to look at the final two chapters in *Lessons for Women*: lessons on how to get along with father-, mother-, brothers- and sisters-in-law. Both include statements on the saying 'nobody can be faultless', for example what the mother-in-law says can be wrong. Ban even admits that the flaws and mistakes a daughter-in-law has made can be well hidden if she is able to live in harmony with others in her husband's family. This proves that the challenge for a wife with respect to her husband's family is mainly a matter of positioning herself in the labyrinthine complex of human relationships in the in-laws' house. In addition, she confirms that wives have their own sense of right or wrong, although Ban sees it as dangerous for wives to exercise such judgement when they are in a situation in which they are completely overpowered. Therefore, it is reasonable to think that the main purpose of Ban's writing is to provide future brides with a set of skills necessary for survival in the hostile world of the in-laws' house. Accommodation, rather than overt confrontation, is viewed as a politically expedient way of dealing with powerful superiors.

The Confucian text *The Great Learning* states that family must be put in order first, and only then can the state be ruled. As a result, strict regulations for the relations between man and woman were set out in Han Confucian texts. Scholars therefore tended to stress the rules for establishing a stable family life and undisturbed continuation of the lineage. This was, at least in part, a reaction to the dissolution of old feudal loyalties and the growth of a new intermediary class that sprang up with the rise of the Western and early Eastern Han dynasties as a new empire. This intention can be easily discerned in *Lessons for Women* as well. For example, Ban advises that enticements like using flattering and coaxing words should be avoided, and that it is best for wives to exercise self-cultivation, suppress contempt and keep a safe distance from their husbands.

However, the thinkers in that bright age did not resolve to learn from the Confucian classics alone. Under the patronage of emperors who were themselves lovers of literature and art, the great literary achievements of the Classical Age of Ancient China, including the teachings of several important schools of thought during that period, were re-edited and reissued in terms more suitable to the new age. In addition to the orthodox works of the Confucians, the *Book of Han* includes 993 sections on works by thirty-seven different authors of the Daoist school and eighty-six sections on the works by six different writers of the Mohist school. Therefore, it should be emphasised that Han philosophy did not derive its conceptions from any single tradition, but from a synthesis of various streams of the pre-Qin schools of thought – mainly Confucianism, Daoism and Mohism.

Ban's family history and the trajectory of her education were at the centre of this trend of thought. Thus, we should question the validity of a solely Confucian interpretation of her life and her texts. Instead, the gender relations and patriarchal values in the texts should be put into context. Here, it is meaningful to note that the palace cult of the Han rulers was predominantly Daoist. Daoism, unlike Confucianism, makes no assumption of the benign nature of man's living environment. The Daoists regard self-preservation and survival as man's first order of business in life, and humility and self-denying service to the strong are seen as necessary skills if men are to negotiate their relationship in a perilous environment.

However, the usefulness of *Lessons for Women* as a historical source is comparatively limited. First, Ban's prescriptions were exceptional even in her own day. Second, remarriage of women was not an uncommon phenomenon. Third, no earlier references stipulate that women were not allowed to speak their minds, and the interdiction of socialising between men and women did not seem to exist or be enforced strictly. Fourth, if we look at those liberal works on sexual life during the Han dynasty – for example, 'Tong Sheng Ge' ('Song of Harmonious Sounds' or 'Song of Love') by Zhang Heng (78–139 CE), who in this poem makes reference to *Su Nv Jing* (*Sutra of Native Woman*), one of the most important works on sex in ancient China – Ban's ideal of womanhood remained the wishful thinking of orthodox Confucian householders for many centuries to come.

In 2017, a series of university lectures delivered by Ding Xuan, a member of the China Women's Development Foundation and executive vice-president of the Hebei Province Traditional Culture Research Association, stirred heated discussions on social media. In one of her lectures about 'being a gentle and graceful woman in the modern era', she argued that 'a woman's best dowry is her virginity' and criticised women for wearing revealing clothing. That such public speeches recur and become a social focus is not a surprising case in today's China. But it does partly prove the relevance and significance of Ban Zhao and her scholarship, even if we disagree with her view. She is an important, influential thinker who deserves our attention and continued engagement.

Hypatia

c. 350–415

Lisa Whiting

When asked to imagine the world of ancient philosophy, most people would think of a group of old men with beards and togas. A woman giving lectures in the public square, attracting large crowds of people who had travelled great distances to hear her speak, would be unlikely to fit into most people's conception. This is one of the many reasons why Hypatia of Alexandria is such a fascinating figure.

Hypatia was a mathematician, an astronomer and a philosopher. She is one of the first philosophers who was both a woman and who has reliable historical records documenting major elements of her life. Despite this fact, many myths surround her. Through the centuries since her death, she has become a central figure in poetry, literature, art and even a Hollywood blockbuster, *Agora*, starring Rachel Weisz. These fictions, though entertaining, have led to significant confusion about Hypatia's life and work. It is important to peel back these layers so that we can appreciate Hypatia for the woman that she really was.

Hypatia was born around 350 CE (although the exact date is unknown) in Alexandria, Egypt, which at that time was part of the Roman Empire. For context, this was around 400 years after the birth of another famous Alexandrian woman, Cleopatra VII. The city of Alexandria was known for its scholarship, second only to Athens, and students would travel great distances to be taught by academics in the city. Theon, Hypatia's father, is thought to have been the head of the prestigious university in Alexandria named the Mouseion. Theon was a famous mathematician and teacher who edited many mathematical works throughout his life, his most notable contribution being an edited early version of Euclid's *Elements*. The book set out extensive fundamental principles of early mathematics, and extracts of Theon's commentary are still in use today. Sadly, nothing is known of Hypatia's mother and no records refer to her.

Theon taught Hypatia mathematics and philosophy from an early age, and sources attest that she soon outshone him. The fifth-century Byzantine historian Socrates Scholasticus wrote in his *Ecclesiastical History* of 'Hypatia, daughter of the philosopher Theon, who made such attainments in literature and science, as to far surpass all the philosophers of her own time'. In terms of her mathematical achievements, Hypatia edited and wrote commentaries on various mathematical texts, including books in Ptolemy's *Almagest*. It was in this text that Hypatia made her most notable mathematical contribution through devising an improved method of long division described as a tabular method. She also wrote commentaries on Diophantus' thirteen-volume *Arithmetica*, devised a new edition of *Handy Tables* by Ptolemy and wrote a commentary on Apollonius' book on the geometry of conic sections. In addition to her mathematical writing, she was also known to build astronomical instruments, such as astrolabes, which were devices used to calculate the position of planets.

As none of Hypatia's philosophical texts have survived, it is not known whether she devised any original theories. However, academics consider it unlikely because during the period it was more common for scholars to comment on existing works and to develop their predecessors' arguments, rather than write original theses. Some speculate that this was due to a desire to preserve existing texts, following the destruction of the famous Library of Alexandria when a significant number of ancient works were destroyed. It is for this reason that Hypatia is regarded more as an accomplished mathematical commentator than an innovator.

Why, then, should Hypatia be considered an accomplished philosopher? To answer this question we must look to her teaching, as it was here that Hypatia truly flourished. Multiple historical sources attest to the popularity of her lectures on philosophy, which were attended not only by enthusiastic students but also by the political leaders of the day. One of her students, Synesius of Cyrene, so admired her work that he wrote letters to her addressed simply to 'The Philosopher'. In one letter to a friend he wrote that Hypatia was 'a person so renowned, her reputation seemed literally incredible. We have seen and heard for ourselves she who honourably presides over the mysteries of philosophy'. Synesius would often send young men great distances to Alexandria to be taught by Hypatia.

Occasionally Hypatia's students' appreciation would turn into more than intellectual admiration as her beauty led many young men in her classes to fall in love with her. She, on the other hand, was having none of it and reportedly remained a virgin until she died. In one famous encounter described by the Platonic philosopher Damascius, Hypatia tried to stifle one of her most persistent student's affections by playing a musical instrument for hours in the hopes he would get bored. When this did not work she turned to more extreme measures and one day pulled out a bloodied menstrual rag and waved it in the boy's face, proclaiming that it was only lust that he desired, and this was not beautiful compared to her intellect and the true wonder of philosophy. Perhaps unsurprisingly, Hypatia succeeded in halting the young man's advances after his soul 'was turned away by shame and surprise at the unpleasant sight, and he was brought to his right mind'.

When she was not teaching in a classroom, Hypatia would go out into the public square to lecture. Historical sources describe Hypatia 'putting on the philosopher's cloak although a woman and advancing through the middle of the city'. She was known to publicly teach the work of Plato, Aristotle and other philosophers to any who wished to listen. This would have been common behaviour for male philosophers of the time, but it was unusual for a woman to teach in public in this way. That Hypatia was so revered for her teaching by countless students serves as a testament to her remarkable talents, not only in philosophy, but also as a charismatic and diplomatic speaker who commanded respect through her intellect.

Hypatia's popularity was also partly due to her openness and inclusivity towards a variety of different people and perspectives. Although a pagan herself, she accepted and taught many Christians and Jews, which was significant given the rising religious tensions of the period. Her student and friend Synesius went on to become a Christian bishop, and another one of her closest confidants was a man named Orestes, who was the governor of Alexandria. Through these relationships she built a reputation as a highly influential political figure, with leaders often asking for her wisdom when facing challenges in their work.

Hypatia was therefore far more than an academic and a talented mathematician; she was a public intellectual who used her role in society to make a positive difference through the connections she made. Damascius describes this well when he says:

> Hypatia's style was like this: she was not only well-versed in rhetoric and in dialectic, but she was as well wise in practical affairs and motivated by civic-mindedness. Thus, she came to be widely and deeply trusted throughout the city, accorded welcome and addressed with honour.

Tragically it was this civic-mindedness and her influence amongst the powerful that eventually led to her brutal death, which is not a tale for the faint-hearted. From around 382–412 CE the Pope of Alexandria was a man named Theophilus, who maintained a good relationship with Hypatia, despite their different beliefs. However, after Theophilus died, his nephew Cyril fought to take power of the city. One of Cyril's critics was Hypatia's friend Orestes, who asked for her advice in dealing with the conflict. Rumours sprang up amongst Cyril's supporters that Hypatia was at fault for Orestes and Cyril's inability to reconcile their differences, which was leading to greater violence in the city. Shortly after these rumours began, a group of monks called the Parabalani raided Hypatia's carriage while she was travelling. The mob stripped her naked and tore her body to pieces using what is translated from Greek as either oyster shells or roof tiles, before dragging her limbs through town. They then set her remains on fire.

Hypatia's vicious murder sent shockwaves through Alexandria, not only due to its violent manner but also because, up until this point, philosophers were considered untouchable figures in city life. The murder had its desired effect by further destabilising Orestes' supporters, and soon after Cyril took complete control of the city. Debate remains around whether Hypatia's murder was ordered by Cyril or if it was an act that arose because of the wider anxiety and violence Alexandria was enduring at the time. Regardless, it is clear that Hypatia's status and influence made her a target.

As the first known female martyr to philosophy, Hypatia's dramatic legacy has often been co-opted to support or denounce various causes. In the early modern period Hypatia was the focus of a book by John Toland, dramatically (and lengthily) titled *Hypatia: Or, the History of a Most Beautiful, Most Vertuous, Most Learned, and Every Way Accomplish'd Lady; Who was Torn to Pieces by the Clergy of Alexandria, to Gratify the Pride, Emulation and Cruelty of their Archbishop, Commonly, but Undeservedly, Stil'd St. Cyril*. Toland's clearly exaggerated view of Hypatia's life made its way into the rest of the book where he made up stories about her to advance his anti-Catholic cause. Thomas Lewis later wrote an essay to rebut Toland's work. Seemingly inspired by Toland's penchant for the dramatic, Lewis titled it 'The History of Hypatia, a most Impudent School-Mistress of Alexandria: Murder'd and torn to Pieces by the Populace, in Defence of Saint Cyril and the Alexandrian Clergy. From the Aspersions of Mr Toland'. In both texts we see Hypatia reformulated into feminine stereotypes that wilfully ignore the reality and complexity of her existence.

In 1853, Charles Kingsley wrote an extremely popular novel about Hypatia which made her a well-known figure with wider, less academic audiences. In 1908, the American writer Elbert Hubbard wrote what he claimed to be a biography of Hypatia's life. However, the book is littered with fiction and involves numerous unsubstantiated claims. Books of this sort contributed to an illusory, romanticised construction of Hypatia, and proliferated numerous myths about her life, many of which remain to this day.

In the twentieth century, Hypatia was adopted by the rising feminist movement. Dora Russell, wife of the philosopher Bertrand Russell, wrote a book discussing the inequality of education between men and woman called *Hypatia or Woman and Knowledge* (1925). The prologue of the book reads: 'Hypatia was a university lecturer denounced by Church dignitaries and torn to pieces by Christians. Such will probably be the fate of this book.' Russell's point – that even thousands of years later academia is still a male-dominated space where women are often taken less seriously – is one of the main reasons Hypatia's legacy is so significant. She was one of the first women to successfully break into the academic sphere that had been largely reserved for men.

Hypatia also saw philosophy and society to be inextricably connected. She taught and made important contributions to advancements in mathematics, but she also used her knowledge and diplomacy for the benefit of society. She could have stayed within the classroom and libraries, teaching and writing and living a quiet life, but instead she chose to speak up and use her political influence for good, a risk that would eventually lead to her death.

Beyond the fiction, we know that Hypatia was an intelligent, charismatic and brave woman. She was likely a leading teacher of her day, as well as a significant public figure in Alexandria due to her civic-mindedness. My hope is that she inspires more women to take the risk, put on the philosopher's cloak and walk out into the square.

Lalla

1320–92

Shalini Sinha

Lalla was an unorthodox figure in the philosophical and social world of fourteenth-century Kashmir. This was a period of transition in which a primarily Hindu and Buddhist philosophical, religious and political context gave way to Islamic influence and political power. Here, Lalla emerged as a universal figure, claimed historically by both Hindu and Muslim traditions.

She is an authoritative individual in the Sufi Islamic tradition as well as the Śaiva Hindu traditions of Kashmir. She is called Lalleshwari by Hindus and Lalla Arifa by Muslims, while her non-sectarian, popular names are simply Lalla or Lal Ded. Her poems, relayed orally for over 600 years, have left a powerful and pluralist legacy in the Kashmiri religious and cultural landscape.

Not only is Lalla one of the most influential figures in the religious history of Kashmir, she is also a well-known figure in Indian classical poetry. In this wider tradition, her rejection and critique of social and religious orthodoxy parallels that of several other well-known women philosopher-poets of classical and early modern India, such as Akka Mahadevi (twelfth century, Karnataka), Janābāi (thirteenth century, Maharashtra) and Mirabai (sixteenth century, Rajasthan), as well as dissenting male philosopher-poets such as Kabir (fifteenth century, Uttar Pradesh). Like these poets, Lalla defies conventional norms in a quest for liberation. In her work she highlights the possibility of a mental and bodily freedom that is accessible to all, regardless of caste, creed or gender. In popular biographies, she, like Akka Mahadevi, is often depicted as a naked ascetic – someone who lived a life of severe self-discipline – who invited criticism for her rejection of convention. Yet, much like other radical female poets, Lalla gained an iconic status that created and legitimised a space for unorthodox feminine poetry and practice.

Tradition holds that after renouncing her home and family at the age of twenty-six, Lalla underwent a period of education in 'non-dual' Śaiva philosophy and its yogic practices. After this training, Lalla wandered the Kashmir countryside as a yogini, a female practitioner of philosophical yoga. The rich philosophical and yogic contents of Lalla's poems bear testimony to this and make it all the more surprising that contemporary scholarship often views Lalla as primarily a *bhakti* or devotional poet, rather than as an accomplished philosopher-practitioner of the Kashmiri Śaiva tradition and its yogic-tantric practices. Her legacy is evident in the varied collection of popular poetry that is attributed to her, which is unlikely to be the work of a single individual and rather expresses the voices of poets of varying religious affiliation, gender and occupation, as Ranjit Hoskote points out in *I, Lalla: The Poems of Lal Ded* (2011).

Lalla's poetic utterances (*vākhs*) evoke the philosophy of the tenth- and eleventh-century non-dual Kashmir Śaiva schools. These schools were deeply indebted to the Buddhist schools of

Kashmir. This branch of Śaiva philosophy is considered non-dual because of its claim that the ultimate nature of reality is beyond the necessarily 'dualising' constructions of thought, concept and language. Lalla's use of terms such as *śiva* (ultimate reality as 'still' awareness) and *śakti* (the vitality or energy of awareness) reflect her Śaiva beginnings, while her use of words such as *śūnyatā* (emptiness) provide evidence for clear Buddhist influence. An emerging tradition of Sufi Islam is also found in her poetry, some of which may be attributed to later additions.

For Lalla, as for most practitioners of philosophical yoga, philosophy is a practice, a search for truth and freedom that requires a radical transformation of body, mind and awareness. This is achieved by undergoing philosophical training in non-dual Śaiva philosophy and its practical realisation in yogic training of mind and breath. Such physical training aims to develop this philosophical understanding as a reality by making it a part of behavioural expressions in everyday life. This non-dualism forcefully rejects the divisive, hierarchical and exclusionary categories that organise contemporary social life. These social, ethical and religious categories form our experiences in terms of high and low, self and other, purity and impurity. This rejection of orthodox thinking is expressed in Lalla's use of a variety of yogic-tantric practices that are ordinarily considered 'impure' and subversive of traditional values and behaviour. These ranged from consuming meat and alcohol, to yogic traditions undertaken in the cremation ground to overcome the fear of death, as well as erotic sexual practices.

Combined with yogic cultivation of mind and breath, tantric or spiritual exercises aim to transform our ordinary perception and understanding of who we are and the nature of the world around us. They do so by attempting to dissolve the conceptual structures that organise our lives and our experience in the world as one of division, moving between the opposing ideas of good and bad, high and low, right and wrong, the forbidden and unforbidden, and so on.

Lalla thus argues that we should overcome the entrenched social, emotional and moral divisions and hierarchies whether of the body, mind or world. She claims that these divisions trap us behaviourally, morally and cognitively and that yogic understanding and exercises are essential for freeing awareness from the conceptual fabric that clouds it. Her poems present the ways we can break down these embedded conceptual dualities of inclusion and exclusion, inner and outer, high and low, and how this can radically change our sensory, cognitive, bodily and social behaviour (v. 61). Here, her dismissal of religious divisions is evident when she refers to the divine using a variety of popular Buddhist and Hindu names, such as Jina and Keśava. On overcoming emotional and moral divisions, she says:

> Good or bad, I'm happy to welcome both
> I don't hear with my ears, I don't see with my eyes . . . (v. 91)
> They lash me with insults, serenade me with curses.
> . . . untouched I move on. (v. 92)

Reflections on the nature of freedom are pervasive in Lalla's poetry. Freedom for Lalla is recognition of the freedom of one's own awareness. Freedom *is* self-recognition, a recognition of our true nature as awareness, an awareness whose essence is its absolute freedom (*svātantrya*) and creativity. This timeless awareness of *śiva* has the power, or the 'conceptual power', to manifest itself, by itself, as the world of conscious beings and inanimate objects.

We experience the world of objects, objects that we take to be 'me' and 'not-me', 'inner' (mental) or 'outer' (physical). However, these are simply manifestations of the freedom of awareness. Lalla explains that awareness or consciousness spreads a 'net' of concepts from within, and this infuses all of the outer world and the inner life of each person (v. 105). According to Lalla, the world is nothing but the conceptual 'net of consciousness', or rather a conceptual net of consciousness-energy, since consciousness is inseparable from energy, which it controls or 'rides'. Body and mind, from this perspective, are conceptual constructions which are inseparable from the energies they harness. Yogic mind and breath training, therefore, aim to cultivate recognition of this world of objects, including the self, as the contents of original awareness that are, in fact, nothing other than this awareness itself.

Yogic recognition leads us to understand the world of objects, usually perceived as separate and disparate, as merely made up of appearances of an aesthetic *play* of awareness – a play which is experienced as joyousness and delight. Yogic practices thus strip away the conceptual net that conceals the reality of the world and of ourselves as unobstructed awareness, 'empty' of the concreteness and solidity of objective and subjective objects imposed by the mind (v. 86). They do so by transforming the conceptual energies that manifest as body, mind and world. This requires a transformation of the mind that controls these energies, which Lalla describes as the 'melting' of the mind's habitual and pervasive constructions by intense yogic training of mind and breath (v. 76–77). By training the mind and the vital energies it controls, the yogini realises the empty, non-conceptual nature of awareness as the ever-present nature of everything. This recognition is experienced as the 'flowering' or freedom of awareness (v. 110).

This process of self-transformation is also explained by Lalla as the refining and uniting of the dual conceptual energies, represented as male and female deities (Śiva and Śakti), that constitute the practitioner's mind and body. With the uniting of these dual conceptual energies in our awareness, the division of inner and outer falls away. The yogini is no longer restricted to her mental or bodily identity – she no longer identifies with her mind and body, or any other mental or physical phenomena as 'me' or 'mine'. This is a falling away of conceptual divisions that overcomes all bodily self-identification and concern (v. 43). Non-conceptual awareness of this sort is the same as the experience of emptiness of the sensory world and of oneself. There is a loss of the 'feeling' that either 'I' or the world have a substantial reality, a reality other than and beyond that of the vast space of awareness. The yogini is now free of all conceptual constraints. This is experienced as an 'awakening' or transformation of her mind in which the senses 'fill' their sense objects in a way that yields sensory experience as aesthetic delight, or 'tasting nectar', in the expanse of awareness (v. 76). Lalla describes the dissolution of the conceptualising mind by which everything dissolves, appearing as empty of substance, in the following way:

> *When the mind melts away, what's left?*
> *Earth, ether, sky, all empty out. (v. 73)*
> *When the mind melts away, what's left?*
> *A void [of the mind] mingles with the Void [of awareness].*
> (v. 74)

The experience of emptiness and sensory delight is the realisation that one simply *is* non-conceptual awareness, or *śiva*, an experience which cannot be conceived or expressed in words:

The Supreme Word you're looking for
Is Shiva Yourself. (v. 136)

It is important to note that Lalla's philosophical practice represents a democratisation of tradition. This was achieved through her articulation of complex philosophical thought in simple terms, using images and metaphors from everyday life. Together with an open rejection of social taboos, this allowed her ideas to gain popularity across the social spectrum, among scholars and the non-literate alike. Lalla's philosophy of freedom seeks to dissolve the divisions and hierarchies of religion, caste and class, gender and sexuality, mind and body, self and world. It does so in pursuit of a freedom that is universal and accessible to all, as the very nature of one's own awareness. It is the ability of her philosophy to speak to the very heart of human experience, by evoking freedom as the ever-present possibility of awareness, that invites closer study of her thought and practice. It inspires us to investigate the possibilities of human freedom today, by moving beyond the conceptual borders, divisions and hierarchies that shape our own awareness.

Mary Astell

1666–1731

Simone Webb

In the next chapter you'll read about Mary Wollstonecraft, who you've probably heard of – she's the biggest name that comes to mind when people think about early feminism. You're less likely to be familiar with the subject of *this* chapter, though. Like Wollstonecraft, Mary Astell analysed women's subjugated condition in relation to men and, like her successor, offered considered solutions. Her feminist philosophical treatise *A Serious Proposal to the Ladies* (1694) appeared a century before Wollstonecraft's better-known *A Vindication of the Rights of Woman* (1792). However, Astell's writing isn't limited to her feminist thought: her prolific output includes arguments on theology, metaphysics, epistemology, ethics and the political intricacies of the day. She feels curiously contradictory to modern readers, writing both scathingly and radically about the negative effects of marriage for women in one text, while being a thoroughgoing conservative about existing social hierarchies in another. In the same treatise, you're likely to find witty satire alongside earnest Christian piety.

We don't know much about Astell's life. Unlike several other major women philosophers of the early modern period, such as Lady Anne Conway or Margaret Cavendish, she was no aristocrat – her father was a Newcastle coal merchant. Like most women in seventeenth-century England, she wasn't formally educated. However, she had an intellectually inclined uncle, Ralph Astell, who is thought to have tutored her. He had connections with a group of philosophers known as the Cambridge Platonists, and Platonist influences are visible in her later writing.

Astell's father died when she was twelve, leaving the family in financial difficulty. With her opportunities as a woman being very constrained, and either not wanting or not having the opportunity to marry, Astell moved to London in her early twenties. She was fortunate to receive aid and contacts from the Archbishop of Canterbury, William Sancroft. Soon after this, she began writing. She never married, boldly choosing instead to live alone, forging friendships with other intellectually oriented women in London and receiving their patronage. In 1709, with the support of friends such as Lady Catherine Jones and Lady Elizabeth Hastings, better known as Lady Betty, she opened a charity school for poor girls in Chelsea. Her life was highly ascetic and devout. She died at the age of sixty-three from breast cancer.

But it's Astell's writing rather than her charitable endeavours or personal devotions for which she is known today. Her first published text was Part I of the treatise mentioned earlier: *A Serious Proposal to the Ladies* (1694). Part II followed just a few years later in 1697. She published another of her feminist works, *Some Reflections Upon Marriage*, in 1700, and in the ensuing years notably wrote on contemporary politics and her magnum opus, *The Christian Religion as Profess'd by a Daughter of the Church of England* (1705). This lengthy theological and philosophical text also challenges gendered inequality. Astell urges women to learn and understand the *rational* grounds of their religion rather than simply accepting dogma on authority.

Astell was very much part of the philosophical milieu at the turn of the eighteenth century. Despite the hindrances of her gender, she engaged directly and indirectly with notable thinkers of the day. *Letters Concerning the Love of God* (1695), from the earlier part of her career, comprises a series of letters between her and John Norris, a philosopher little known today but prominent in his time. John Locke is one of the best-known philosophers of the era, and while Astell didn't directly communicate with him, she engaged in detail with his philosophy, sharply criticising his empiricist thought. She also indirectly challenged another contemporary woman philosopher, Damaris Masham (also known as Damaris Cudworth, Damaris Cudworth Masham and Lady Masham), John Locke's friend and companion. In *The Christian Religion*, Astell rebuts arguments that Masham puts forward in her own treatise, *A Discourse Concerning the Love of God* (1696) – albeit under the impression that she's responding to Locke. Masham, like Astell and nearly all women writing at the time, published her work anonymously.

Astell's work was widely read at the time she was writing, although it dropped from view quickly after her death. Intellectual women used her ideas to support their own quests for knowledge by sharing and discussing her books. Despite writing anonymously, Astell's identity wasn't exactly a secret. Her books were well known enough in the late seventeenth and early eighteenth centuries to be satirised by writers like Jonathan Swift (better known today for *Gulliver's Travels*), as well as plagiarised by the famous eighteenth-century idealist philosopher George Berkeley in his compendium *The Ladies Library* (1714).

So, where does Astell stand philosophically? As well as her feminist thinking, which I'll get to shortly, she engages with several key issues of the day. She can be broadly characterised as a Cartesian and a Platonist, meaning that she inherits philosophical stances from the 'father of modern philosophy', René Descartes, and one of the earliest, greatest philosophers of all, Plato. This manifests in a tendency to emphasise the value of the spiritual realm over the material world, and to argue that knowledge gained through rational reflection and contact with divinity is more certain than knowledge gained through sensory perception. In *A Serious Proposal to the Ladies* she argues that we should 'withdraw our selves as much as may be from Corporeal things, that pure Reason may be heard the better; to make that use of our senses for which they are design'd . . . but not to depend on their Testimony in our Enquiries after Truth'. This is in contrast to Lockean empiricism, which sees the mind as a blank slate, or *tabula rasa*, until knowledge is acquired by worldly experience. Indeed, Astell strongly opposes Locke on several important philosophical and theological points. Like Descartes, she argues for the existence of an immaterial, immortal mind which is united in *this* world to a material, mortal body – but which is superior to that body, and worthy of greater care and attention. Unlike Descartes, however, she doesn't believe that the nature of the mind can be known by humans, arguing further that not all minds are the same or have equal capacities. Unequal capacities between minds, however, are not gendered; women and men are naturally equal in rationality and the ability to be virtuous.

In this way, Astell uses Cartesian ideas to support her feminist arguments. If the minds of men and women are essentially the same, there is no reason to bar women from the same education and self-development which men are encouraged to pursue.

Many of Astell's philosophical standpoints shore up her feminist stance like this: her theory of human free will and autonomy, for instance, reinforces her conviction that women are conditioned into *lacking* such autonomy. The growing scholarship on Astell convincingly demonstrates how her positions in different areas interlock, forming a coherent, complex and original philosophical system.

Unlike much later feminist thought, Astell's concern about women isn't that they lack *rights*, or are materially oppressed by a patriarchal society. Instead, Astell shows how women's *selves* are warped and corrupted by social customs and lack of education, making them prone to ethical flaws such as pride and vanity. She writes in *A Serious Proposal*: 'If from our Infancy we are nurs'd up in Ignorance and Vanity; are taught to be Proud and Petulent . . . Humorous and Inconstant, 'tis not strange that the ill effects of this Conduct appear in all the future Actions of our Lives.' Societal sexism makes it difficult for women to become rational and ethical beings.

Her response to this problem isn't to advocate large-scale social change. She maintains that 'men therefore may still enjoy their Prerogatives for us, we mean not to intrench on any of their Lawful Privileges'. Instead, Astell puts forward a two-fold strategy for remedying the problems that women are subject to. First, and most famously, she sets out a proposal for an all-female educational retreat in which women can develop themselves into virtuous, rational beings and form improving friendships with other women: 'One great end of this institution shall be to expel that cloud of Ignorance, which Custom has involv'd us in, to furnish our minds with a stock of solid and useful Knowledge.' Secondly, she outlines an intellectual and moral regimen which individual women can follow to cultivate themselves. By practising philosophical reflection and emotional self-control, women can become *internally* free from the tyranny of social custom and their own emotional fluctuations: 'Our only endeavour shall be to be absolute Monarchs in our own Bosoms.' Astell hopes that her female readers will gain autonomy, even if their legal and social situation remains unchanged.

In addition to *A Serious Proposal*, Astell presents a critique of marriage in *Some Reflections Upon Marriage*, which still reads as radical today. While she accepts marriage as a divine institution and believes that within marriage women do in fact have a duty of obedience to their husbands, she also argues that most marriages are bad for women. Men exercise their authority and power in arbitrary, unreasonable ways, forcing women to submit their rationality and autonomy to unsuitable partners. There's no way out of this once women are married – Astell's strict Christian beliefs hold no room for divorce. However, she implies that for most women it's better if they don't get married at all, writing, 'Perhaps if they took time to consider and reflect upon it, they seldom wou'd Marry.' This subversive argument accords with her advocacy of a separatist women's community in *A Serious Proposal* as somewhere women can be free of male sexual and romantic advances and 'may be kept secure, from the rude attempts of designing Men'.

Astell feels paradoxical. Her feminism stands alongside a deep social conservatism and can often be found wanting. Her proposal for a women's educational space, for instance, is explicitly aimed at women of a certain class and financial means. These are 'Persons of Quality' who are able to afford 'five or six hundred pounds' to put towards the project. Her writing isn't concerned with the oppression of poor and working-class women, and she upholds class-based social hierarchies. She's not exactly an intersectional feminist! You might see her focus on individual self-transformation for women rather than collective resistance as an inadequate response to patriarchal oppression.

Furthermore, she devalues the material body as opposed to the immaterial, immortal mind and soul. This puts her at odds with a strong feminist tradition which re-emphasises the importance of embodiment and interprets the elevation of the mind as containing implicitly masculine ideals. The centrality of her Christian beliefs to her philosophical and feminist framework may not chime well with an increasingly secular readership and a world in which religious institutions and belief systems are often charged with upholding patriarchal power.

Despite these issues, Astell stands out as a woman who was devoted to other women, aligning herself with womanhood and the cause of furthering women's abilities. Although she was largely forgotten shortly after her death, we can find resonances of her ideas throughout the history of feminist thought. Scholars are connecting her work with modern feminist theorising about power, autonomy, trauma and separatism, with recent work even linking her thought to the phenomenon of 'gaslighting'. Some claim her as the first English feminist – a thinker who didn't just point to inequalities between men and women, but theorised those inequalities, called for their remedy and offered solutions. If you want to get to know her work better, get hold of *A Serious Proposal to the Ladies* and dive in; it's as sharp, funny and excoriating as it ever was, and makes a great introduction to this brilliant, underappreciated philosopher.

Mary Wollstonecraft

1759–97

Sandrine Bergès

Mary Wollstonecraft, while not quite a household name, is probably better known than the other women in this collection. While today her fame is due to her fearless defence of women's rights and to her calls for radical educational reform, this recognition is fairly recent. Wollstonecraft was famous for her writings during her lifetime, but the years following her death saw a sharp decline in her reputation, which had more to do with her life choices than with her work (her husband had revealed many personal details in his biography of her). In the early twentieth century she became popular again with feminists such as Virginia Woolf and Emma Goldman, but again it was her life more than her works that attracted their attention.

I first came across Mary Wollstonecraft because a male colleague of mine suggested there weren't enough women on our syllabus for a history of political thought course, and offered *A Vindication of the Rights of Woman* (1792) as an addition. I read the book over the next few days, and have never looked back.

Mary Wollstonecraft was born in London in 1759. Shortly after her birth, her family inherited manufacturing mills from her paternal grandfather. But her father's gambling and drinking meant that by the time Mary was a teenager, the family was quite poor. They moved constantly to avoid creditors and, as a result, Mary's education was neglected. An intelligent and curious child, she took advantage of any library she came across and acquired a fairly solid education for herself (though she did not know Greek or Latin, and her French was not as fluent as she wished). It is fascinating to trace the development of her writing skills through her letters, starting with the poorly spelled and awkwardly phrased teenage correspondence with her friend Jane Arden, in Beverley, Yorkshire, and the subtle, beautiful and incisive letters she wrote about Scandinavia towards the end of her life.

Wollstonecraft's upbringing also provided her with a painful education in what it was like to be a woman in a society when women had no rights of their own. Her father was a violent man who used to beat her mother when he had been drinking. And while Mary's quasi-fictional descriptions of her mother are rather cruel – she complains of her mother's lack of interest in her, and her general apathy – her husband, William Godwin, tells us that the young Mary would camp out in front of her mother's bedroom door, to protect her on nights when her father had been drinking. No doubt this experience of living with a violent father gave her an early understanding of what the dependency of women in marriage could mean. Later in her twenties, her newly married sister complained that her husband was violent and that she could not stay with him. Wollstonecraft immediately orchestrated her sister's escape and, from then on, held herself responsible for her safety.

Perhaps because she had been in charge of educating herself from the start, Mary's first concern as a writer, and one of her first attempts at earning a living, was to do with education. With both her sisters and her best friend, Fanny Blood, Wollstonecraft set up a school for girls in Newington Green, which was then still a village in North London. The school did not last long: Fanny moved to Portugal with her fiancé and became very ill following childbirth. Mary travelled to Portugal to try to help her but Fanny died soon after, and when Mary returned to London, the school was bankrupt. However, the experience was a significant part of Wollstonecraft's life, as much of her writings are concerned with the education of girls.

When the school failed, Wollstonecraft was in debt and her first recourse was to write a book, *Thoughts on the Education of Daughters* (1787), in which she began to develop arguments for greater gender equality in education, in particular where the development of abstract thinking was concerned. She also advocated for young women to travel abroad before they married, arguing that this was how men got an unfair advantage over their wives, having been allowed to experience the world before settling down to build a home and a family. The book sold well. Books on education were popular at the time and Johnson, her publisher, was a specialist in that area. But Mary was still in debt, and in order to pay it off, she taught herself French and took up a position as governess to a Protestant Irish aristocratic family, the Kingsboroughs. She did not flourish in the job, as she resented her employers' superficiality and tyrannical tendencies. She did, however, make a lifelong friend and admirer of one of her charges, Margaret, and she again used her time to observe and build up her store of philosophical ideas. Her frequent comments on the negative impact of aristocratic manners on society in general, and little girls in particular, no doubt came from what she observed in Ireland. Here Mary again benefitted from the loan of a library, and while with the Kingsboroughs she read Jean-Jacques Rousseau, the eighteenth-century French political philosopher who was then famous as much for his novels as his educational and political writings. Inspired by his mixture of autobiography, fiction and philosophy, she planned a book, named after her eponymous heroine, Mary. *Mary: A Fiction* (1788) tells the story of a young woman neglected as a child, but who develops her own intellect through reading and writing. Mary is disappointed first in friendship, then in love, but she settles into a non-carnal love relationship between two souls.

Mary Wollstonecraft got on too badly with her employers to stay with them long. She came back to London and the first person she visited was her publisher, Joseph Johnson. He immediately offered her rooms above his shop and a job as translator and reviewer for his *Analytical Review*, where she stayed from 1787 until 1792. She continued to work for Johnson until her death in 1797.

Working as a publisher meant that Wollstonecraft did not need to seek subscribers before she could write a book. For her contemporaries, this was how they secured a contract with a printer, by gathering enough pledges to buy the book once it was written – very much like a modern-day crowdfunder. Johnson knew what would sell and was keen for Mary to write more educational texts for him. Wollstonecraft's next two books after *Mary: A Fiction* were a collection of readings for young ladies and her *Original Stories from Real Life* (1788), moral tales with a female teacher and her two young charges learning about the world and how to respect others, whether men, women, poor, rich or even animals. Wollstonecraft's commitment to education stayed with her till the end of her life, and her most famous book, *A Vindication of the Rights of Woman*, is in many ways a treatise on educational reforms. Women, she argues, need to be educated in the same manner as men if they are to claim their rightful place in society.

When Edmund Burke attacked her friend and mentor Richard Price in his pamphlet against the French Revolution, Mary wrote the first reply – her *A Vindication of the Rights of Men* (1790). In that book, she first articulated her belief that to be free means to be free from domination, and that therefore it is important to be independent to the extent that one is capable of and able to make one's own decisions. So a French serf before the revolution was dependent because they could not afford to stand up to their master, and because they lacked the intellectual resources to know what it would mean to do that. But equally, a woman whose material life depends on her husband is unfree, even if she does not realise she is, because there are a number of choices she simply could not make for herself without her husband's approval. In that sense, an unequal marriage is as much a tyrannical state as a relation of master and slave. In *A Vindication of the Rights of Men*, Wollstonecraft defended the republican ideals of the French Revolution, arguing that the poor of France were in an intolerable relation of dependence towards the rich, one they could not easily break out of, because part of that relation involved the stunting of their capacity for independent thought. Wollstonecraft's first philosophical fight was thus on behalf of the poor, not specifically women.

Johnson printed her book, though he did not print Thomas Paine's own reply, *Rights of Man* (1791), a few weeks later. It was Johnson who suggested to Mary, when he saw that she was falling into a bout of depression the following year, that she write a defence of women's rights. She did, turning to the question of how republicanism affected women and, in particular, how their (lack of) education prepared them for a life of being dominated. Wollstonecraft, presaging the idea that the oppressed sometimes adapt their preferences to fit their reality, argued that dominated individuals often lose the will to reclaim their freedom. Instead, they come to 'hug their chains' and think of their condition as normal, even sometimes desirable.

Once the second edition of her *A Vindication of the Rights of Woman* was out, it was Johnson again who suggested Mary go to Paris, to write about the revolution.

Mary arrived in Paris at the end of 1792, just as the king's trials were beginning. She wrote that Louis being driven to the courthouse was one of the first sights she witnessed and the horror of the scene, and the dignity of the king, made her cry. In Paris, she met Gilbert Imlay, an American entrepreneur who became her lover. In 1794, she was pregnant by him and registered (falsely) as his wife at the American embassy so as to avoid being imprisoned as an Englishwoman. She moved first to the suburbs for safety and then, after she had given birth to her daughter Fanny, to Le Havre. During her two and a half years in France, she wrote *An Historical and Moral View of the Origin and Progress of the French Revolution* (1794), a review of texts written by revolutionary writers such as Mirabeau, Brissot and Condorcet.

While Mary was writing and caring for her newborn in Le Havre, Imlay was in London, living with an opera singer. When she found out, Mary attempted suicide. In order to help her, perhaps, but also no doubt to get her out of the way, Imlay sent her on a journey to Scandinavia to investigate the loss of a shipment of silver he had smuggled out of France. Mary set off to discover the North with a right of attorney, her infant daughter and a

French maid. While she was there, she penned the *Letters Written During a Short Residence in Sweden, Norway and Denmark* (1796), her social and political as well as aesthetical reflections on Scandinavia.

When Wollstonecraft came back from Scandinavia, her friend Mary Hays introduced her to the philosopher William Godwin, whom she had met once at Johnson's. The two became lovers and in 1797, after she found out she was pregnant, they married. During her pregnancy, she worked on a novel – *Maria; or, The Wrongs of Woman* (published posthumously in 1798) – which some see as the sequel to the second *Vindication*. *Maria* takes up the theme of how domination can harm women, no matter their social background. It tells the story of an aristocratic woman, Maria, married to a tyrannical man who has her imprisoned in an asylum for the insane so that she does not leave him and take her child with her. Jemima, her jailer, is a poor woman who has been abused from childhood and lived on the streets and as a prostitute until, by luck, she was able to educate herself and gain this job. The novel tells how the two women slowly learn to trust each other, looking at what they have in common as well as their differences. During that time Wollstonecraft also started a book on child rearing, which emphasised the equal roles of mother and father, and made notes for another philosophical treatise. She did not complete any of these as she died of puerperal fever in September 1797, ten days after giving birth to her second daughter, Mary.

Fanny Imlay, her first daughter, committed suicide in early adulthood. Mary Godwin inherited her mother's love of writing, travel and her unfortunate predilection for unreliable men. She went on to marry Percy Shelley and write one of the greatest novels in English literature, *Frankenstein*.

Wollstonecraft is not the only philosopher to have argued for women to be better educated, nor indeed that their intellectual abilities are equal to men's. Nor was she the first to decry the social conventions that kept women from becoming what they were capable of being. But she was one of the first to defend such views and to argue that they should be executed now. Hers are not mere suggestions. Whether stories for children or treatises on political philosophy, her writings are always instructions for change to be put into practice now. In that sense she has much more in common with contemporary philosophers such as Martha Nussbaum and Amartya Sen: her job is to change the world, to analyse the causes of suffering and to argue for the best remedy.

Harriet Taylor Mill

1807–58

Helen McCabe

Harriet Taylor Mill's intellectual contribution has been overshadowed for too long by the academic stature of her second husband, John Stuart Mill, despite his best efforts to credit her work as inspirer, discussant, collaborator and co-author.* Dismissal of Stuart Mill's account is often based on personal criticisms of Taylor Mill. Here, I try to clear away some of the fog of dislike and misogyny on the one hand, and Stuart Mill's praise on the other. She was human. She was a woman. She was extraordinary.

Born in London on 8 October 1807, Harriet was the daughter of Harriet and Thomas Hardy (a surgeon), and one of six siblings. She came to strongly disapprove of her parents' narrowly self-interested attitude. Home-educated, she learned several languages, read widely in literature, history and philosophy, and kept up with newspapers and periodicals. Although

---

* Harriet Taylor Mill was never actually her name; she was Harriet Hardy, then Harriet Taylor, then Harriet Mill. But accuracy can, in this case, be confusing.

many of her fragmentary manuscripts and letters bear witness to her complaint that 'my pen will not keep pace with my feelings', her completed works are polished and imposing.

Contemporaries record her as being very beautiful: she had a long neck; an oval face; large, wide-spaced, deep-brown eyes; long dark hair worn up with ringlets framing her face; and the kind of complexion which manages to look good in yellow (as the portrait of her in the National Portrait Gallery shows). But she was also intelligent, passionate, imaginative, incisive, stubborn, loving, thoughtful and sometimes righteously indignant, hating cruelty, unfairness, pettiness and intellectual and emotional dishonesty.

In 1826, she married John Taylor, a twenty-nine-year-old pharmaceutical wholesaler, whom she described as upright and generous, a 'brave and honourable man, of liberal opinions and good education' that she loved with her whole heart. Their eldest child, Herbert, was born in 1827, Algernon (known as Haji) followed in 1830, and finally Helen (known as Lily) in 1831.

Both Harriet and John Taylor were involved in radical politics, moving in the free-thinking circle which came to embrace Stuart Mill. Unbeknownst to his friends, Stuart Mill was recovering from a 'heavy dejection' caused by his losing faith in the reforms he had essentially been bred to achieve by his father James Mill and the renowned utilitarian Jeremy Bentham. Taylor Mill wrote: 'The whole foundation on which [his] life was constructed fell down' and he despaired of finding a 'power in nature sufficient to begin the formation of [his] character anew'. Such a power he found in Harriet.

Stuart Mill seems to have been as much of a thunderbolt across the summer sky of her life as she was a lightning flash across the darkness of his. They soon fell deeply in love. Although Taylor Mill tried to sever ties with her husband, Stuart Mill protested:

their paths, he wrote, 'though parted, can, and must, meet again. This is not the end'. And it was not.

Taylor Mill wrote many pieces on marriage, women's rights, women's education, and the power of society over the individual, particularly women's moral character and happiness at this time. Her analysis is nuanced, sophisticated and original. She separates sex from what we now call gender, explaining how the latter, though deep-rooted in women given their education from birth, is a social construct, and identifies core elements of what would now be termed the patriarchy. She strongly critiques the powers exercised by husbands over wives, and the insidious power of society to shape – and warp – the individual mind. She advances bold claims regarding the real nature of marriage (bartering sex for subsistence), the wrongness of the current marriage vows, the impossibility of divorce, and legislating for expressions of affection between consenting adults; and the importance to happiness of self-development, individuality and enjoyment of life rather than ascetic rejection of it. Controversially linking sex with morality, she writes:

> Sex in its true and finest meaning, seems to be the way in which is manifested all that is highest best and beautiful in the nature of human beings . . . Who extends and refines those material senses to the highest . . . best fulfils the end of creation. That is only saying – Who enjoys most, is most virtuous.

It is still debated whether she and Mill put this philosophy into practice. But in late September 1833 Taylor Mill acted on at least some of her views, separating from her first husband. Given the constraints of the period – with no right to legal separation, access to her children or any financial support, and almost no means of earning her own living – this was an enormous step. Stuart Mill soon joined her in Paris, where they could finally realise how perfectly happy they made each other. But there remained, as Stuart Mill outlines in a letter, 'all the other obstacles, or rather the one' to continuing this happiness for 'the rest of [their] natural lives' – John Taylor, and their three children.

Taylor Mill knew that she and Stuart Mill were not the only people whose happiness ought to be considered. Determining to act on her ethical principles, and to try to maximise the happiness of everyone involved, she returned to London – to a sexless marriage, and back to a platonic relationship with Stuart Mill.

She did not remain long living in her husband's house – a decision which forced her into social isolation. She was also plagued by ill health, including partial paralysis. However, during the next decade and a half, Taylor Mill wrote some short pieces on ethics and religion, and discussed Stuart Mill's work, culminating in suggesting the need for an entire chapter in his *Principles of Political Economy* (1848) and setting the whole 'tone' of the book by persuading him that, though the laws of production might be 'fixed' (like the laws of gravity), the laws of distribution are mutable human constructions. This realisation means that the existence of rich and poor is suddenly not a settled fact of either nature or religion, but the outcome of human (in)activity. Thus, workers demanding reform cannot be fobbed off with the excuse that things can't be changed; it has to be proved that this is the best possible social arrangement.

Improvements and alternatives to the status quo are considered in the chapter of *Principles* taken from Taylor Mill's lips. There, she and Stuart Mill outline how workers' increasing demands for independence will lead to their rejection of wage-relations with capitalists in favour of profit-sharing schemes, and eventually their rejection of any form of dependence on capitalists at all, instead setting up producer and consumer cooperatives. Through a gradual process of organic, piecemeal change, all private property would end up in the hands of worker-run and managed cooperatives, and we would have arrived in a socialist future which would be 'the nearest approach to social justice, and the most beneficial ordering of industrial affairs for the universal good, which it is possible at present to foresee'.

Principles cemented Stuart Mill's reputation as one of the leading minds of his day. He tried to give public credit to Taylor Mill in the dedication, but, according to his autobiography (1873), her dislike of publicity prevented this. There was soon a second edition, in the preparation of which Taylor Mill was deeply involved.

In 1849, John Taylor became seriously ill. Taylor Mill moved back into his house, and fought tirelessly against his disease and apathy, but to no avail.

Now formally free to marry Stuart Mill, they faced the obstacles of his family's disapproval, and their own feminist objections to marriage, outlined in Stuart Mill's 'Statement on Marriage' (1851). Despite this, they wed in 1852. During this period, Taylor Mill wrote and anonymously published *The Enfranchisement of Women* (1851), an extended argument for female suffrage, and fragments which would eventually be included in *The Subjection of Women* (1869), Stuart Mill's famous penetrating critique of the socially constructed oppression of women. Later in the decade, she and Stuart Mill worked together on his autobiography, a series of articles on domestic violence, and *On Liberty* (1859).

On Liberty is generally viewed as Stuart Mill's greatest contribution to political philosophy, and ought to be counted as Taylor Mill's as well. It is perhaps one of the clearest and most passionate defences of freedom of speech ever written. It contains a comprehensive defence of personal liberty – its core claim being that people may only be forcibly prevented from doing as they see best if they cause harm to others. This is a strongly anti-paternalist stance: *On Liberty* is adamant that a person's own (supposed) good can't be used as an excuse to force them to do something against their will. There is also a strong perfectionist element: *On Liberty* passionately defends the importance of self-created, self-developed 'individuality'.

Unfortunately, Taylor Mill's health was failing. She died in Avignon on 3 November 1858, one year before *On Liberty* was published. The book began with this dedication:

> To the beloved and deplored memory of her who was the inspirer, and in part the author, of all that is best in my writings – the friend and wife whose exalted sense of truth and right was my strongest incitement, and whose approbation was my chief reward – I dedicate this volume. Like all that I have written for many years, it belongs as much to her as to me . . . Were I but capable of interpreting to the world one half the great thoughts and noble feelings which are buried in her grave, I should be the medium of a greater benefit to it than is ever likely to arise from anything that I can write, unprompted and unassisted by her all but unrivalled wisdom.

Stuart Mill died in a house overlooking Harriet's grave in 1873 and was buried with her.

The circumstances of Harriet Taylor Mill's life and times mean her contributions to politics, economics and philosophy went under-recognised and undervalued by her contemporaries. It is time for us to do better.

George Eliot (Mary Anne Evans)

1819–80

Clare Carlisle

George Eliot is an undisputed queen of English literature, but she also deserves a place in our philosophical tradition. She was born Mary Anne Evans in Nuneaton in 1819 and died Mary Anne Cross in London in 1880. For much of her adult life she wished to be known as Mrs Lewes, due to her long-term partnership with the writer George Henry Lewes. Yet when she began to write fiction in the 1850s, she assumed the male pseudonym of George Eliot. She felt that her novels would not be recognised as the serious philosophical contributions they were if they were known to be authored by a woman.

Like Maggie Tulliver, the passionate, scruffy heroine of *The Mill on the Floss* (1860), the young Mary Anne had a voracious intellectual appetite. Her curiosity and spiritual sensitivity soon led her beyond the horizons of her conservative lower-middle-class Anglican family. In her teenage years she was fervently religious, then during the 1840s she became friends with a group of free-thinkers near Coventry and reached the conclusion that Christianity was based on 'mingled truth and fiction'. Throughout her life she prized 'wide' (one of her favourite adjectives) outlooks, open minds and expansive souls, over what was narrow, hard and petty. Despite her shining intelligence and remarkable aptitude for learning, she could not study at Oxford or Cambridge, or at London's newly founded University College or King's College. It was not until much later in the nineteenth century that a university education became possible for even a small number of women in England.

So, before she became George Eliot, Mary Anne Evans undertook a self-tutored philosophical apprenticeship. While reading Spinoza in 1843, she wrote to her friend Sara Hennell that 'We cannot fight and struggle enough for freedom of enquiry.' Her interests ranged widely, encompassing new scientific theories and the history of religion. She translated two recent German works, both crucial turning points in nineteenth-century Christianity: Strauss's *Life of Jesus* in 1846, and Feuerbach's *The Essence of Christianity* in 1853. She also translated Spinoza's *Ethics* from Latin in 1856 (and she had translated at least part of Spinoza's *Theological-Political Treatise* in the mid-1840s, though that manuscript has been lost).

In 1851, changing her name to the more sophisticated Marian, she moved to London to become the unofficial editor of *The Westminster Review*. This was an unprecedented role for a woman, and one that placed her inconspicuously at the heart of English intellectual life. Her numerous articles for *The Westminster Review* gave her opportunities to comment not only on new literature, but also on contemporary social issues. These included what Victorians called 'the woman question': the place of women in a deeply patriarchal society that was becoming gradually receptive to ideas of gender equality.

It was through her fiction, however, that George Eliot made her most significant contribution to philosophy. The genre of the novel gave her a wide canvas for exploring questions about freedom and responsibility, moral weakness and empowerment, and, of course, the development of character. In the series of novels that brought her wealth and fame – *Adam Bede*; *The Mill on the Floss*; *Silas Marner*; *Romola*; *Felix Holt, The Radical*; *Middlemarch*; and *Daniel Deronda* – she showed that these are not abstract questions; they are lived by embodied men and women who are ensconced in complex social worlds, and driven by material cares, emotional needs and spiritual desires. Eliot's stories elaborate a philosophical view of human beings as irreducibly themselves, yet also deeply impressionable. Although her characters are often moulded by entrenched habits, she portrays people as constitutionally open to change and new growth. Perhaps this is most clear in the development of Silas Marner from a poor 'withered' creature with a merely 'mechanical relation to the objects of his life' to a loving and beloved father and friend. Like 'a handle or a crooked tube', the narrator comments, a human being 'has no meaning standing apart'.

European philosophers in the nineteenth century often responded to the great works of Immanuel Kant, which in many ways set the agenda for modern philosophy. Samuel Taylor Coleridge's dissemination of Kant early in the new century had a powerful influence on the generation of English writers which Eliot followed, and she also engaged closely with German thought herself. While ambitiously metaphysical thinkers, such as Schelling and Hegel, sought to overcome the dualism in Kantian thought between deterministic natural laws and absolute moral freedom, Eliot focused on ethical and psychological questions. She agreed with Kant that religion finds its justification in ethical life – a view developed by Feuerbach, whose ideas she knew well and admired – and she shared Kant's distrust of speculation about God and related metaphysical questions. Yet whereas Kant saw morality as regulated by reason, she followed the Romantics' tendency to emphasise feeling. She was particularly interested in the deep moral (and indeed redemptive) feeling of 'sympathy' between two human souls – an empathic connection she dramatised repeatedly in her novels.

Eliot also differed from Kant in rejecting his ideal of rational autonomy. She saw human beings as profoundly interdependent, reciprocally shaped by their encounters and relationships. In the 'Finale' to *Middlemarch* (1872) she declared that 'there is no creature whose inward being is so strong that it is not greatly determined by what lies outside it.' She may have drawn this insight from Spinoza's *Ethics*, though she certainly made it her own. Her characters show that life is always interactive; they are shaped by their family ties, friendships and social relationships. Eliot is sometimes wrongly perceived as a typical Victorian moralist, but in fact she was a moral philosopher in the broadest sense. She was concerned above all with human flourishing, and was keenly aware of all the complexities and difficulties this involves.

In her last novel, *Daniel Deronda* (1876), Eliot reflected that 'Men, like planets, have both a visible and an invisible history. The astronomer threads the darkness with strict deduction, accounting for every visible arc in the wanderer's orbit; and the narrator of human actions, if he did his work with the same completeness, would have to thread the hidden pathways of feeling and thought which lead up to every moment of action.' She wrote of this book that 'I meant everything in the book to be related to everything else there.' Through the literary form of the novel, Eliot accomplished a deeply philosophical task: bringing into view the interconnectedness of a human world. She showed the intricate links between ecological, social, political and psychological forces, often by drawing analogical relations between characters and events. When we read her novels, we find ourselves in the curious imaginative situation of being at once inside the web of a fictional world – we feel affected by what happens there, and our interpretations and our sympathies flow into it – and outside the web, surveying it as a whole. The narrator of *Middlemarch* describes herself as 'unravelling certain human lots, and seeing how they were woven and interwoven' – and as she accomplishes this 'seeing', so do we. In this way, Eliot's fiction helps to guide us through what Socrates saw as the essential work of philosophy: knowing ourselves.

Like Spinoza, Eliot believed that self-knowledge brings about a kind of liberation, even though external circumstances always remain beyond our control. Moira Gatens, a feminist philosopher and Spinoza scholar, has described George Eliot as 'a determinist who nevertheless believed in freedom and the expansion of knowledge through human striving'. Eliot often showed her characters gaining greater understanding of themselves, and thereby becoming more contented. For example, the carpenter Adam Bede finds that his experiences of suffering and love deepen his understanding, giving him a sense of 'enlarged being' and 'fuller life'. As Adam puts it, 'It's a feeling as gives you a sort o' liberty.'

Eliot also depicted many characters failing to understand themselves and others. In *Daniel Deronda*, for instance, the proud and beautiful Gwendolen Harleth has to decide whether or not to marry Grandcourt, a wealthy man whom she does not love. Eliot shows us the combination of causes that leads

Gwendolen to accept her suitor, and enter willingly into a miserable, destructive marriage: she misunderstands Grandcourt's character; she seeks a solution to her family's financial troubles; she wants to ensure her mother's security; she longs for attention, material comfort and social status; her pride makes her recoil from becoming a governess, the only alternative prospect offered to her. Gwendolen is mistaken not only about Grandcourt, but also about the nature of human freedom. At the beginning of the novel, she believes that being free means getting her own way. One of her reasons for agreeing to marry Grandcourt is her ill-judged expectation that he will, as her husband, do 'entirely as she wishes' – and thus she becomes subject to *his* tyrannical wilfulness. Though Eliot does not offer her a conventional happy ending, through her mistakes and her friendships Gwendolen eventually begins to appreciate the spiritual freedom that comes through self-understanding.

The philosophical depth of Eliot's writing distinguishes her from other great novelists of her age. This is exemplified in her treatment of marriage, which was, of course, a central trope in many nineteenth-century novels. In Eliot's hands, it became much more than a plot device providing readers with a feel-good 'happy ending'. She approached marriage as a site for serious reflection on the human situation. In her novels, as in life itself, marriage is a meeting place for nature and culture, bodily and spiritual desires, public and private life, the romantic and the quotidian, choice and compromise, passion and restraint, empowerment and interdependence. For Eliot's heroines, the challenge is not simply to find and keep the right man – as in Jane Austen's novels – but to find the right way of being married.

Although Eliot's approach to social questions sometimes appears rather conservative, she was acutely attuned to the difference between living in harmony with one's family and neighbours, and meek adherence to stifling social norms. She drew on her own romantic experience, which was complex and unconventional, to reflect deeply on the question of how to find domestic happiness without being confined by it. Among her most successful characters are women who manage to steer a middle way – not a compromise, but a deeper path – between convention and non-conformity. In *Adam Bede* (1859) Dinah Morris, a young itinerant Methodist preacher, finds that her non-conformist life distances her from her family and takes her away from the village which offers her a home. Her relationship with Adam teaches her that romantic love need not be a temptation that draws her from her true vocation. Getting married and settling down enables Dinah to channel her 'power of loving' in a way that strengthens the whole community.

Eliot also puts before her characters the challenge of finding a middle way between egotism and self-denial. Her heroines Dinah Morris, Maggie Tulliver, Romola de' Bardi and Dorothea Brooke all try earnestly to master their selfish desires, yet they cannot flourish while repressing themselves. The tragedy of *The Mill on the Floss* is that Maggie finds no resolution to this dilemma; having exhausted both possibilities, she has nowhere to go, except down into the depths of the River Floss. For Dinah and Dorothea, marriage proves to be a middle way between selfishness and self-denial, just as it is a middle way between adhering to social norms and rejecting them. Romola, by contrast, has to decide whether to leave a husband who is unfaithful and morally corrupt. Eliot proposes no easy solution and, instead, she shows Romola realising that she is confronting the deep moral problem of 'where the sacredness of obedience ended, and where the sacredness of rebellion began.'

Recognising George Eliot as a powerful philosophical voice not only enhances her reputation, it enhances philosophy too by giving feminine experience more weight than many established philosophical texts allow it to have. It encourages us to accept that emotional intelligence is crucial to the task of understanding what it means to be human, and how to live a good life. It also reminds us that the wisest philosophers are those who help us to see why life can be so difficult and complicated, and who situate moral questions where they belong: within the tangle of human feelings and human relationships.

Edith Stein

1891–1942

Jae Hetterley

To the non-philosopher, Edith Stein's life outside her philosophical career is perhaps better known. Born to a Jewish family, she became an atheist in her teenage years before converting to Roman Catholicism as an adult. After her time in academia she became a nun, and shortly before the Second World War began she was transferred to a monastery in the Netherlands for her safety. Following a statement from Dutch bishops in 1942 condemning Nazi racism, a crackdown on Jewish converts to Catholicism ensued, and she died at Auschwitz, most likely on 9 August 1942. Today she is one of six co-patron saints of Europe.

In philosophy, Stein is a more marginal figure than she perhaps ought to be. During her short philosophical career, she was part of one of the most exciting philosophical movements of the twentieth century – phenomenology. This was the movement that also included or inspired other famous philosophers such as Martin Heidegger, Hannah Arendt, Jean-Paul Sartre and Simone de Beauvoir.

Stein was only the second woman in Germany to earn a philosophy PhD. Her supervisor was Edmund Husserl, the founder of modern phenomenology, and she took a job as his assistant.

To understand Stein's work, we first need to understand phenomenology. Most simply, phenomenology aims to centre first-person descriptions of human experience as philosophically enlightening. Husserl's most famous formulation is as a response to radical scepticism; that is, the age-old question of how we can find grounds for our knowledge insofar as it is possible to doubt all of our beliefs. For Descartes, overcoming scepticism involved recognising one undoubtable belief to form the foundation upon which the rest of our knowledge could be built – *I think, therefore I am*. However, Husserl took a different tactic, reasoning that even if I can doubt the veracity of all my experience, what I cannot doubt is *that* I experience. Therefore, philosophy can circumvent scepticism if it enquires into the nature of experience *as it is experienced*. Husserl aimed to overcome scepticism by taking it out of the picture. To remove scepticism was to reorient philosophical inquiry towards the structures of experience ('intentionality') and away from the question of knowledge.

A characteristic of phenomenology is in showing how our natural attitudes to given philosophical problems don't cohere with the results of our reflections on the nature of our intentionality – and Stein's early work follows this trajectory. A key focus of her PhD was on the problem of other minds. Given we don't have access to each other's mental states, how can we know for certain that others have mental states like our own, or indeed that others have mental states at all? The traditional response to the problem is that we *infer* the existence of other minds. That is, in our social interactions, we see that others have similar responses to us: we all shout if we're angry, or laugh if we find something funny, or stop paying attention if we're bored. Because of these similarities, I can infer by analogy that others have minds just like my own. But Stein did not think this was the case, arguing instead that we know other minds through the experience of *empathy*. In this, Stein makes the characteristic phenomenological move that when we reflect on our experience, we see that the entire taxonomy of social interaction is different from what the traditional response suggests. For an inference to be required, it would mean we'd need to undergo some leap in knowledge – from seeing a physical body to concluding it has mental states. But we *don't* have an experience of someone's mental states as distinct from their physical body because it's all one entity. We don't experience bodies and states, we experience *persons*, and for Stein, an empathetic experience is one where the other is already given *as a person*. Here we recognise not a physical body which we need to infer has a happy mental state like our own; rather, we recognise a happy person.

Stein's thought, therefore, can be characterised as heavily influenced by Husserl, but she was not a mere disciple. For instance, where Husserl ultimately came to view phenomenology as a form of transcendental idealism (that the objects of our experience are in some way mind-dependent), Stein's work suggests she was resolutely a realist. Furthermore, following her conversion to Catholicism, she began to engage with philosophy of religion and theology in a way that Husserl's work never attempted, and her book *Finite and Eternal Being* (1950; written once she was a nun) was an explicit attempt to combine phenomenology with scholastic metaphysics and theology.

Stein's key development is in arguing not just that knowledge of other minds is already given, but that it is given through an experience of empathy, through direct recognition of the other as a person. And these notions of direct access, of disputing philosophical taxonomies through first-personal reflections, are resolutely phenomenological methods.

Husserl saw phenomenology as a collaborative project, akin to a science; of a group of philosophers working together in different phenomenological domains but within the same basic structure. And indeed, once Stein completed her PhD and became Husserl's assistant, she was at the heart of the phenomenological project. Here is where the uncomfortable realities of being a woman in philosophy reared its head. Stein's main task upon becoming Husserl's assistant was to take his notes on the phenomenology of time and work them into a publishable manuscript. These texts were a disparate collection: a set of lectures from 1905, plus some earlier and later notes, and even some more contemporary articles (which Husserl may have provided to help Stein).

Stein's work involved going well beyond what would ordinarily be expected of an editor. Husserl hadn't written a first draft for Stein to provide suggestions or do some surface rewriting to tidy the manuscript up. Rather, she set to work on the disparate materials, evening them out, changing their order to construct a coherent philosophical narrative until *she* had a first draft. Much of the correspondence from Husserl's students, Stein included, shows how his working attitude was often quite fickle. He would often get obsessed with particular philosophical problems for brief (but intense) periods, often to the detriment of his students, and it would only be after Stein had completed the first draft that he became enthusiastic about the project. But then Stein's contract came to an end, and she had to make a decision about her future. She wanted to complete her habilitation – a necessary qualification for holding a permanent academic chair and supervising PhD theses in Germany – but Husserl rejected her submission. In the end, she left the secular academy and taught at Catholic institutions. When the Nazis came to power in 1933, she was forced to resign from her position there too.

For a decade, the manuscript on time was left untouched. For all that Stein had done to forge her own path within the phenomenological school, Husserl's dismissal of her habilitation effectively cut her career short. It is difficult to be certain of the exact reason but given her close collaboration with Husserl over a number of years, it seems extremely unlikely that it would be the quality of her work, not least because in 1928, Husserl published the manuscript she had worked on as *On the Phenomenology of the Consciousness of Internal Time*. The work is credited to Husserl, and its supposed editor, Martin Heidegger. Now, it is true that the book was published as part of the *Yearbook of Philosophical and Phenomenological Research*, of which Husserl and Heidegger were co-editors, and so Heidegger would have had a hand in readying the manuscript for publication – but a much more substantial part of the philosophical legwork was Stein's. If she hadn't been tasked with working up Husserl's notes into a manuscript, there would be no manuscript. And yet the only credit that she received in the text itself was a note inserted by Heidegger saying that she transcribed Husserl's stenographic lecture manuscripts.

It is difficult to ascertain how much of the work is Stein's and how much is Husserl's – but without a doubt, she deserved better. And all of this, we should note, was not even uncovered until the 1991 English translation appeared, in the introduction by John Barnett Brough, the translator. In the end, Stein's academic career was stymied because of Husserl's sexism – and later on, the Nazis' racist legislation – but also because Husserl and Heidegger would not even credit her for the work that she did.

In many ways, Stein's short period in academia speaks to the way women's achievements in philosophy are not only downplayed, but sometimes entirely ignored. And for all that philosophers like to think we are objectively searching for necessary and universal truths – unaffected by the contingency and bias of ordinary life – in fact, philosophy is never done in the abstract, and neither can philosophers be apart from the contingencies of our particular time. Many consider the popular image of the philosopher to be harmless – and yet that image is reflective of the dominant political forces of its time. It is a white, male and heterosexist image. And this isn't some ivory-tower politics: in Stein's case – and indeed, for many other women and minoritised groups in philosophy – there are material effects that the image engenders. On one level, Husserl and Heidegger have to share responsibility for their actions in Stein's specific case (even while they were entirely unaccountable in their lifetimes), and yet on the other, we have to consider the institutional hurdles which can still be in place that allow such actions to continue to go unchecked – and even if one wants to concede that things are somewhat better today, we still have to ask why there are so few minoritised groups in academic positions in philosophy departments.

History cannot be rewritten, and what happened to Stein cannot be undone – but what we can do is create a more welcoming and diverse academic environment, in which the voices of marginalised groups do not continue to be marginalised, where we challenge the complacency of philosophers' self-image in our own work, and we incorporate voices such as the women in this collection into our curricula. Insofar as philosophy ought to be engaging with the world in which it is written, there is still much to be done.

Hannah Arendt

1906–75

Rebecca Buxton

The Origins of Totalitarianism (1951), Hannah Arendt's most famous political work, was difficult to find in book-shops across America in November 2016. This major treatise on anti-Semitism, imperialism and totalitarianism sold out across the US after the election of President Donald Trump. Writing on the nature of totalitarian rule in Nazi Germany, Arendt described a group of people typically forgotten by politicians. She wrote, 'Potentially, they exist in every country and form the majority of those large numbers of neutral, politically indifferent people who never join a party and hardly ever go to the polls.' She could easily be writing about the present day.

Born to a German–Jewish secular family in modern-day Hanover, Arendt grew up as an only child with a keen interest in learning. Her mother's detailed diaries told of a 'sunshine child' who read whatever she could access. When Arendt's father was dying of syphilis during her early childhood, she would sit with him and play cards well into the evening. After her father died, Arendt became a companion to her mother. Although they were happy together, Arendt later lamented her fatherless childhood. However, out of this lonely youth and love of books grew a deep affection for philosophy.

In a famous television interview with Günter Gaus on *Zur Person* (1964), Arendt said, 'I always knew I'd study philosophy . . . I read Kant. You may ask why I read Kant. For me the question was either I study philosophy or I drown myself.' She indeed went on to study philosophy, with a minor in theology and Greek, at the University of Berlin. She later moved to Philipps University of Marburg, where she was tutored by the well-known continental philosopher Martin Heidegger. Arendt is often only mentioned in reference to her romantic relationship with Heidegger, a notable thinker who later joined the Nazi Party. In 1929, after her relationship with Heidegger ended, Arendt married Günther Stern (better known by his later name of Günther Anders), a fellow student of Heidegger.

Arendt predicted that the Nazis would come to power, years before it became obvious to most political analysts. In 1933 she became heavily involved in anti-Nazi organising and was soon detained by the Gestapo for compiling evidence of anti-Semitic hate speech. She was held captive for eight days, but escaped by befriending her jail guard whom she described as 'charming'. Arendt was then smuggled to France by a Zionist organisation. Here Arendt's circle of friends reads as a who's who of the European intellectual elite. She frequently spent time with Walter Benjamin and here met her second husband, the poet and philosopher Heinrich Blücher.

Arendt was not interested in politics and history in her early years. Asked later when she became engaged in politics and political theory, she replied with an exact date: 27 February 1933 – the burning of the Reichstag and the illegal arrests of Jewish people in Germany. From that moment, Arendt said, she felt responsible. In 1937, after several years in Paris, Arendt was stripped of her German citizenship and became stateless. In 1940, French authorities rounded up illegal Jewish German refugees, described as 'enemy aliens', and sent them to internment camps. Arendt was taken to Gurs but later escaped during the chaos of the Nazi invasion of France. She soon fled to Portugal and then, in 1941, travelled to America with Blücher on an illegal visa – she would only become an American citizen many years later. Her mother, Martha, was initially denied a visa to America and followed her daughter several months later. Arendt had never been in an English-speaking country, but she mastered the language quickly and began writing once again.

Arendt went on to become one of the most influential and controversial political theorists of the twentieth century. Interestingly, she rejected the label of 'philosopher', and may have objected to being included in this book altogether. She instead thought of herself as a political theorist, arguing that there was a constant tension between philosophy and politics. In the case of politics, she argued, it is not possible to be neutral, even for the well-trained philosopher. She was also far from a self-professing feminist. Instead she argued that 'it doesn't look good when a woman gives orders'. However, in her actions, Arendt often ensured she was not kept in what she considered to be a woman's position. She stated, 'I always did what I wanted to do, I never cared if it was a man's job.'

After her life in Germany and France, Arendt continually advocated for thinkers to focus on lived experience rather than abstract political concepts. She wrote in her 1960 essay 'Action and the Pursuit of Happiness', 'I have always believed that, no matter how abstract our theories may sound or how consistent arguments may appear, there are incidents and stories behind them which at least for ourselves, contain in a nutshell the full meaning of whatever we have to say . . . Incidents of living experience must remain its guideposts by which it takes its bearings if it is not to lose itself in the heights to which thinking soars or in the depths to which it must descend.' Indeed, Arendt felt that her Jewish identity had always affected her thinking. She was clear about the impact of the Holocaust on her work. In that same television interview she said, 'The decisive day was when we heard about Auschwitz. Before that, we said: "Well, one has enemies. That is natural. Why shouldn't people have enemies?" But this was different. It was as if an abyss had opened. Amends can be made for almost anything at some point in politics, but not for this.'

Arendt's writings are difficult to group into a single, coherent theory. Her central focus was the nature of politics and political existence. Her discussion of how totalitarian governments gained power, outlined in *The Origins of Totalitarianism*, still resonates today. In its most basic sense, she argues that totalitarianism arises when people are disconnected from each other. A political movement then emerges and offers a story which claims to explain why people are unhappy. This story becomes so powerful that it creates an overwhelming narrative with which people cannot disagree. She calls this 'the rule from within'. Totalitarianism takes over people's minds and by extension the whole of society.

Arendt's second argument on totalitarianism shows the influence of Aristotle. She argues that there are two parts to a human being: their biological being, or their body, and their political being. Totalitarian regimes succeed when they reduce people to their body and strip them of all of their social and political identity. In *Why Read Hannah Arendt Now* (2018) Richard Bernstein summarises Arendt's theory of totalitarianism, arguing that its ultimate aim is 'to make human beings as human beings superfluous'. Totalitarian nation-states did so by destroying human spontaneity and individuality. This destruction of human beings as political actors, Arendt argued, allows whole groups of people to be killed without causing public uproar, just what happened in Europe during the Second World War.

Although Arendt never offered any solutions to the rise of totalitarianism, she was interested in the nature of political communication. In particular she considered the ways in which citizens ought to engage in political life, taking her lead from many of the early Greek city-states. Arendt was a huge admirer of Socrates, whom she believed to be a philosopher par excellence. She therefore considered open debate and discussion of ideas. A well-developed political community is one that listens to one another's political ideas and has a culture of forgiveness for those who make mistakes. There has to be a conversation and a marketplace of ideas; an argument which we should surely be learning from today.

Arendt's work has also received greater attention because of the recent so-called 'refugee crisis'. As a stateless person for many years, she argued that the situation of displaced people tells us much about the function of nation-states, as well as how humans can achieve meaningful political action. Shortly after escaping to America, Arendt published a defiant essay, 'We Refugees' (1943), in a small Jewish journal. In her usual confident tone she began, 'In the first place, we do not like to be called "refugees".' She went on to argue that optimism for displaced people in Europe during the Second World War was unfounded – instead, the European people had allowed 'its weakest members to be excluded and persecuted'. In *The Origins* Arendt discussed what she called 'homelessness on a massive scale', arguing that refugees and state-less people, and indeed all people, have 'the right to have rights'. However, she was highly suspicious of abstract human rights, believing that these rights can only be guaranteed by *belonging to a place*. Everyone needs access to relevant political institutions in order to have their rights guaranteed. Writing on the mistreat-ment of displaced people across Europe and North America, she concluded that 'what is unprecedented is not the loss of home but the impossibility of finding a new one.' Refugees and state-less people were excluded from accessing the political institutions that would enable them to exercise their rights and were there-fore, according to Arendt, rejected from humanity altogether. The parallels with today are simple to draw. Many displaced peo-ple are excluded from access to legal protection and still do not have 'the right to have rights'. For much of her life Arendt was likewise a citizen of nowhere. She instead belonged to what she called in 'We Refugees' a new kind of human being in contem-porary history: 'the kind that are put in concentration camps by their foes and internment camps by their friends.'

When Arendt died of a heart attack in 1975, she was per-haps best known for her essays written for *The New Yorker* on the Eichmann trial, published in 1963. Otto Adolf Eichmann, a Nazi lieutenant colonel, arranged the removal of millions of Jewish people to concentration camps throughout the Second World War. Eichmann faced a widely publicised trial for war crimes in Jerusalem in 1961. He was found guilty and executed in 1962.

Writing on the trial in her usual blunt and often ironic tone, Arendt faced huge controversy after this publication. She introduced here the idea of 'the banality of evil', arguing that Eichmann was not sociopathic or driven by extreme ideology, but instead an extremely average person who relied on cliché as his primary defence. The banality here is not that Eichmann's actions were ordinary or to be considered normal, but that his actions were motivated by a lack of thought or ideology altogether. She maintained that he simply looked like a civil servant who had had no internal moral conversation about his actions; he was a thoughtless bureaucrat. At the time, many argued that this focus on banality trivialised the murder of millions of Jewish people during the Holocaust. However, Arendt maintained that she clearly distinguished between the deed and the doer – the fact of the Holocaust, Arendt maintained throughout all of her writing, was unforgivable. She was not claiming that his action was banal. Instead, she claimed that Eichmann's evil was a privation of thought. These issues became personal for Arendt, with members of the public sending abusive letters and trying to have her volume of the essays, *Eichmann in Jerusalem: A Report on the Banality of Evil* (1963), barred from publication. This late controversy coloured public opinion of Arendt throughout her later life until her sudden death at the age of sixty-nine.

A final comment should be made about Arendt's racism. In her writings she repeatedly refers to Africa as 'the dark continent' and describes its inhabitants as 'savages' and 'barbarians'. In her controversial essay 'Reflections on Little Rock' (1959), Arendt characterises Black parents fighting for the desegregation of schools in the American South as 'social parvenus', aiming to gain access to the higher classes through forcing their children into all-white schools. In her book *Hannah Arendt and the Negro Question* (2014), Kathryn T. Gines (now Kathryn Sophia Belle) takes Arendt to task on her inconsistent treatment of Jewish oppression and African-American marginalisation in the US. Most writers on Arendt don't comment on her racism. Those who do often argue that we should focus on her thought instead of her character. Such a reaction doesn't seem right – particularly given her own emphasis on lived experience. This is an issue for philosophy and political theory more broadly, one that certainly requires more careful treatment than I can give it here. For now, let us be reminded that no thinker should be idolised above criticism. Instead, we need to acknowledge such shortcomings and evaluate them, just like we evaluate Arendt's political theory.

In spite of these controversies, Arendt is remembered above all as a dissenting intellectual who refused to blindly accept prevailing opinion. She was often disliked for her sarcastic and ironic writing style, as well as her sharply successful critiques of mainstream political theory and philosophy. Her experience as a stateless person unquestionably shaped her writing and should continue to mould how we discuss and address statelessness today. Though she may not have considered herself a philosopher, she deservedly sits in this volume as one of the greatest political thinkers of the twentieth century. I hope she wouldn't mind our including her.

Simone de Beauvoir

1908–86

Kate Kirkpatrick

Western philosophers have a long history of using prison metaphors to describe the human condition. The Gnostics described the body as a prison, offering knowledge of salvation to those who could resist the temptations of the flesh. Before them, Plato thought human beings were prisoners of their ignorance, like cave dwellers who mistook shadows for reality. For Rousseau, society itself held men captive: 'Man is born free,' he wrote, 'and everywhere he is in chains.' Simone de Beauvoir had a prison metaphor, too. But it was not the *human* condition that she thought it described – it was the 'feminine condition'.

Her prison metaphor was a harem – a place where women were kept in positions of submission to men in order to magnify their greatness and satisfy their pleasures, instead of being free to pursue projects or pleasures of their own. She used this to challenge one of the twentieth century's most famous philosophers – Jean-Paul Sartre – about his concept of 'human' freedom throughout the 1930s, before they rose to joint fame as a legendary intellectual couple after the Second World War. Then, she challenged him in print – and went on to write one of the best-selling books in the history of philosophy: *The Second Sex* (1949), which reputedly passed the million-copy mark in the 1980s.

Both philosophically and biographically, it is tricky to write about Beauvoir without discussing Sartre. (I can almost hear the shoulders of my feminist readers tighten as they read that sentence, but bear with me.) For much of the twentieth and even twenty-first century Sartre's reputation as a philosopher overshadowed Beauvoir's and she was falsely described as having 'applied' Sartre's philosophy in her own works. The fact of the matter was that she publicly disagreed with him (and many others), forged her own version of existentialism, and eventually changed Sartre's mind. So why did she think that 'the feminine condition' was one of captivity and submission?

As a student Beauvoir set national records: at twenty-one, in 1929, she was the youngest person ever to pass the aggregation exam in philosophy, and only seven women before her had ever passed it. Fortunately for posterity, Beauvoir's student diaries (from before she met Sartre) were preserved and published in French in 2008. They show that even as a teenager Beauvoir was preoccupied with 'existentialist' philosophical questions. She was fascinated by the nature of freedom and how she could become an ethical self, voraciously reading in search of a philosophy that she felt could do justice to life – intellectually and practically. She was raised in a religious household, with a secular father and Catholic mother, and exposed to both Christian and humanist ethics. Both traditions venerated 'love' as an ideal, whether ethical or romantic. But at an early age Simone noticed that where love was concerned, different expectations applied to men and women.

At home her father famously said that Simone had 'a man's brain', that she 'thought like a man'. He also thought that women couldn't be truly creative, in the sense of having originality or genius. The young Beauvoir noted that he was in the company of many philosophers: Schopenhauer's 1851 essay 'On Women' called women 'the second sex, inferior in every respect to the first', claiming that while it was possible for women to have talent, they could never have 'genius'. Whether from her father's lips or philosophers' pens, Beauvoir grew up in a culture where girls were expected not to shine too brightly, because the glare of too much genius might scare suitors away.

She would later develop existentialist ethics, employing an original philosophical method in *The Second Sex*, win prestigious literary prizes for her novels, and campaign for lasting reforms to French law. But her successes came at a cost: she was the target of spite and scorn, frequently reduced to the role of 'Notre Dame de Sartre', a woman whose fame could be attributed to the genius of the man beside her.

The question of which work is Beauvoir's first *philosophical* work is itself a philosophical question. Her first published work was a novel, *She Came to Stay* (1943). The phenomenologist Maurice Merleau-Ponty would praise this as a new way of doing philosophy in fictional form, showing life unfolding in the concreteness of characters' consciousness. But novels can be interpreted in multiple ways, and philosophers who want 'philosophy' to consist of clearly defined views and well-argued theses are usually reluctant to assign fiction the same status.

Readers didn't have to wait long, however, for Beauvoir to publish her views in a more traditional philosophical form. In 1944 Beauvoir published an essay, *Pyrrhus and Cinéas*. This work is still little known in English (although it was published in English in 2004), but here Beauvoir developed her existentialist ethics. The previous year Sartre had published a massive tome of philosophy entitled *Being and Nothingness*, which painted a bleak view of human relationships. Sartre claimed that the essence of interpersonal relationships was conflict, and that love was an unrealisable ideal. In two philosophical essays from the 1940s Beauvoir described *Being and Nothingness* as a 'failure' and existentialism as a philosophy that did not 'imply an ethics'. Beauvoir therefore introduced her own work as providing the ethics that existentialism lacked. But despite this, for much of the twentieth century her role in the development of existentialism was widely overlooked.

In *Pyrrhus and Cinéas* Beauvoir asked ancient philosophical questions: Why do something rather than nothing? What does it mean to 'love your neighbour as yourself'? Beauvoir believed that humans have no Platonic essence, Epicurean fate or divine calling that determines them to be what they are. When a human being looks at her future, she has to choose between many possible selves, and *act* in order to become one of them. As an existentialist, Beauvoir was committed to the view that human beings are defined by their actions, continuously becoming over time, through pursuing different *projects* that shape us. But she disagreed with Sartre about the extent to which we are free to choose who we become.

In *Being and Nothingness* Sartre claimed that human beings are radically free, and that no matter what projects we've previously decided to pursue – where a project could be being a writer or a philosopher, or loving a particular person – at any point we are free to renounce that project and pursue another. But Beauvoir did not think our past becoming could be so easily renounced. And she didn't think that all members of society could so easily renounce the external expectations that conditioned the selves they became.

In the mid-1940s Beauvoir and Sartre emerged as an iconic power couple of post-war Paris. Beauvoir gave lectures in America and France on the state of women writers, and on the new philosophy 'existentialism'. At this time she was not fully aware of her own privilege; she found it irritating that people asked her to summarise existentialism in a single sentence when they would never expect to understand Kant or Hegel in such a perfunctory way. Despite its growing reputation as a popular philosophy, Beauvoir claimed that to really understand existentialism you needed to understand the entire philosophical tradition behind it. But she continued to develop her existentialist ethics, arguing in *The Ethics of Ambiguity* (1947) that it was inconsistent to value one's own freedom without valuing the freedom of others.

It is in this period that *The Second Sex* was developed. During her travels to America, Beauvoir observed that the relationship between the sexes was very different there than in France. And she saw first hand the way race divided America, with her mixed-race friends Richard and Ellen Wright. She read a book called *An American Dilemma* (1944), by the Swedish sociologist Gunnar Myrdal, in which Myrdal argued that race relations in America were trapped in something like – but importantly unlike – a vicious cycle. He called this dynamic 'the principle of cumulation': Black people were seen to be inferior, kept in positions of subordination, and did not achieve the same successes as their white compatriots, so their white compatriots concluded that they were by nature inferior and incapable of achieving success.

In *The Second Sex* Beauvoir wanted to write a book as important as *An American Dilemma* – but on women. The result was a massive, two-volume work. The first volume studied the man-made 'myths of woman': she surveyed biology, history, psychoanalysis, economics, religion and literature to show that women are often defined as man's 'Other'. In the second volume, she employed an original phenomenological method, drawing on many women's voices to show first-person perspectives about girlhood, adolescence, puberty, sexual initiation, pregnancy, motherhood, marriage, ageing and more. Taken together, they were a testament to the ways women suffer as a result of the man-made 'myths of woman'.

In the 'feminine condition', Beauvoir thought that to become a woman was to become a 'split subject', torn between recognising one's own freedom and living up to externally imposed ideals. Becoming a woman 'in the present state of culture and education' was to be inducted into inferiority, to a world in which women were taken by nature to be secondary and submissive to men. The problem, as Beauvoir saw it, was that women were not inferior by nature. Since the eighteenth century Diderot and many others had assigned responsibility for women's inferior status to society. The question, as Beauvoir saw it, was whether this situation had to be perpetuated.

Beauvoir believed that it did not, but in order for women's situation to be improved both men and women would have to recognise and redress their complicity in its perpetuation – both would have to learn to see women as subjects, not objects. For too long, Beauvoir wrote, women had been expected to dream through men's dreams, in public and private life. Beauvoir argued that previously philosophers such as Husserl, Sartre and Merleau-Ponty failed to take into account experiences particular to the female body, and the ways that, for women, being embodied involves being objectified – being 'prey' to the desires of men, wanted or not. To become a woman was to become an object to be seen, not a subject to be heard.

Beauvoir also returned to the concept of love, claiming that love meant different things for men and women. For men, love was part of life. But for women, love was often portrayed in history, philosophy and literature as though it was life itself. Women were expected to sacrifice themselves for their beloved in a way that was not reciprocal. Developing on her earlier ethical claim that to value your freedom you must also value the freedom of others, in *The Second Sex* she claimed that authentic love involved mutual recognition of the freedom of both lover and beloved, in a relationship of reciprocity.

When *The Second Sex* was published Beauvoir was subject to vitriolic and highly personal attacks on her character. She had made a philosophical argument about the oppression of women, and rejected the analyses of many influential male writers as partial because they only described the world from a limited point of view: the point of view of some men. In this respect, Beauvoir is an excellent example of a dynamic that Virginia Woolf wryly observed in *A Room of One's Own*: the consequences of being critical are not the same for women. Writing in 1929, Woolf wrote that it is impossible for a woman to say 'this book is bad, this picture is feeble, or whatever it may be, without giving far more pain and rousing far more anger than a man would do who gave the same criticism.'

But Beauvoir's work did more than provoke anger – it provoked change. Beauvoir dreamed of being a writer whose words would 'burn in a million hearts'. As a student she loved philosophy passionately, but she thought that there were two types of metaphysicians: those who valued abstract philosophical systems and those who valued the subjective experience of human beings. She was the latter, and for much of her career she chose to write literature because she thought that by showing human beings in concrete situations – even if they were fictional – her readers could undergo 'imaginary experiences' that helped them re-see their place in the world.

Throughout the 1940s and early 1950s Beauvoir wrote several more novels, including the one that won the prestigious Prix Goncourt, *The Mandarins* (1954). But in the mid-1950s she became convinced that she had been guilty, like many intellectuals, of keeping her cultural privilege to herself. She believed that existentialism was a philosophy that should be lived. And although she had written 'existentialist' novels for those readers who did not have the elite philosophical educations to *really* understand existentialism, she thought that the message of *The Second Sex* was too important to be accessible only to those who could read 800-page philosophy books.

So Beauvoir wrote something in a different genre. In 1958 she published *Memoirs of a Dutiful Daughter* in which she applied the theory of *The Second Sex* to her own life without the jargon of philosophy or psychoanalysis. It was a huge success – hundreds of ordinary French women wrote to her saying that she had 'come down from a pedestal'; some even wrote to chastise her for writing *The Second Sex* in a way that only the Paris literati could follow. Over the next few years, Beauvoir continued to write her life in story form. After the publication of these memoirs readers went back to *The Second Sex* to try to better understand their own situations – and it was only then that second-wave feminist movements started to form in France.

In later life Beauvoir continued to write fiction, life-writing and philosophical works; she knew her pen was a powerful weapon against oppression. But she was no longer content to provide 'imaginary experiences' of liberated women in her novels; she campaigned for legislative reforms that would give women

concrete freedoms in the world. Alongside the feminist movements she helped to inspire, she pursued changes, including con-
traceptive rights and divorce law reform as well as laws prohibiting
sexualised images of women. In word and in deed, she fought for
women to be able to see themselves as 'the eye that sees' the world,
as free subjects whose desires and pleasures should shape it – not
just as objects to be seen.

Iris Murdoch

1919–99

Fay Niker

Many know Iris Murdoch either primarily or exclusively as a novelist. She published twenty-six novels, starting with *Under the Net* in 1954, selected as one of the Modern Library's 100 best English-language novels of the 20th century, and ending with *Jackson's Dilemma* in 1995, the year before she was diagnosed with Alzheimer's disease. Her prolific, distinctive prose – which characteristically wrestles with philosophical themes such as good and evil, sexual relationships, morality, and the power of the unconscious – made her one of the most revered novelists in post-war Britain and, as a result, a Dame Commander of the Order of the British Empire.

Dame Iris was also a moral philosopher by training and trade, holding the position of tutorial fellow in philosophy at Oxford University (1948–63) and continuing to publish influential works later in life, most notably *The Sovereignty of Good* in 1970. For many years, Murdoch's literary success was thought to have surpassed her achievements and influence as a philosopher. This view is now shifting. Recent scholarship has traced the substantial, even transformative, influence of Murdoch's distinctive thought on Anglo-American philosophy; and contemporary thinkers are returning more and more to her prescient writings, finding within them a rich resource for grasping the complexities of our lives as moral beings. Hence, her influence as a philosopher seems to be more dynamic than her distinction as a Booker Prize-winning novelist: her philosophical legacy is being recovered from the past and continues to grow.

Murdoch was born Jean Iris Murdoch in Dublin, Ireland in 1919, the only child of Anglo-Irish parents. The family moved to London when she was an infant in order for her father to take up a clerk position in the Ministry of Health, though they often returned to Ireland. In the introduction to *The Red and the Green* (1965) – her ninth novel, set in Dublin during the week leading up to the 1916 Easter Rising, which explores the complex interrelations between an Anglo-Irish family who differ in their religious and political affiliations – Declan Kiberd writes that Murdoch, 'like many Anglo-Irish before and after her, came to know the strange condition of declaring herself Irish in England while feeling herself to be English in Ireland'. However, her Irish identity marked her deeply; in an interview for *The Paris Review* in 1990, Murdoch stated, 'I feel extremely Irish.'

Murdoch excelled in her schooling at Badminton (a boarding school in Bristol), and went to Somerville College, Oxford in 1938 to read 'Mods and Greats', a degree comprised of Greek and Latin literature, ancient history and philosophy. It was here, while the Second World War raged in Europe, that she became friends with Philippa Foot, Mary Midgley and Elizabeth Anscombe. This remarkable generation of women philosophers, which also produced Baroness Mary Warnock, is thought to have been, in part, made possible by the relative absence of men within the student body on account of the war. In a letter to the *Guardian* in 2013 entitled 'The golden age of female philosophy', Midgley wrote: 'As a survivor from the wartime group, I can only say: sorry, but the reason was indeed that there were fewer men about then.'

Recently, it has been suggested that these four women philosophers should be viewed as a unique and previously unrecognised case of an 'all-female philosophical school'. As evidence for this, Clare Mac Cumhaill and Rachael Wiseman of the In Parenthesis project at Durham University refer us to the fact that, in the years following the war, these women met regularly at Philippa Foot's house to discuss the ambitious project of setting out 'a detailed and comprehensive philosophical response to the dominant conception of human nature, perception, action and ethics in Modern Western philosophy'. A passing look at their many notable publications testifies further to this interconnection: Midgley wrote the foreword for Murdoch's *The Sovereignty of Good*; Foot dedicated her *Virtues and Vices and Other Essays in Moral Philosophy* (1978) to Murdoch, her one-time lover; and Murdoch dedicates her *Metaphysics as a Guide to Morals* (1992) to Anscombe.

The five years between graduating and returning to philosophy were formative for Murdoch. For the remainder of the war years, she worked at the Treasury in London (1942–44) and, more significantly, as an administrative officer with the United Nations Relief and Rehabilitation Administration (1944–1946), first in Belgium, where she briefly met Jean-Paul Sartre in 1945, and then in Austria. According to Peter J. Conradi, Murdoch's friend and biographer, her witnessing the breakdown of human society in Europe, and the capture and execution of her first great love, Frank Thompson, by the Nazis in 1944, 'hurt Iris Murdoch into moral philosophy'. When she returned to philosophy – first with the Sarah Smithson studentship at Newnham College, Cambridge in 1947 and then as a fellow at St Anne's College, Oxford in 1948 – her attention was directed towards defining 'the Good with a view to conducting our lives in its light.' Her distinctive view on this expresses an important facet of the broad, alternative approach to moral philosophy that the wartime group sought, and successfully established.

Murdoch rejects both of the dominant approaches to morality of her time. The first was the Anglo-American analytic philosophy of her Oxbridge contemporaries. Philosophers such as R. M. Hare and Stuart Hampshire were also deeply marked by their wartime experiences. Hare was a prisoner of war for three years under the Japanese, while Hampshire interrogated Nazi officers at the end of the war, convincing him that evil existed. They responded by forming and contributing to the 'muscular choice-is-all school of moral philosophy'. This claims both that the moment of ethical choice, issuing in overt action, is the core of our moral life, and that the will is the central mechanism in choosing the appropriate action. The second approach was Continental existentialism, associated most prominently with the work of Jean-Paul Sartre and Simone de Beauvoir. Murdoch's first book (and, impressively, the first book published in English on Sartre's philosophy) was *Sartre: Romantic Rationalist* (1953). Existentialism, too, focuses on matters of will and choice, arguing that moral values are not fixed but rather created through our choosing will. Despite their differences, these dominant schools of 'modern' moral philosophy in the 1950s and 1960s rested on the same view of human nature; it's this fundamental moral-psychological picture that Murdoch thinks is mistaken and philosophically distorting.

Her rival picture sought to capture the importance of our *inner life* for moral action. Murdoch began this task in 'Vision and Choice in Morality' (1956), and then set out a more mature version in *The Sovereignty of Good*, especially the first of the three papers collected therein entitled 'The Idea of Perfection' (originally published in *The Yale Review* in 1964). Morality, properly understood, is at least as much a matter of 'vision' as it is choice. What does Murdoch mean by this? Briefly put, there is a moral reality external to the agent that was absent in the choice-is-all picture. This recognition shifts the focus of our primary task as moral agents, to *seeing* or *perceiving* the moral features of this world of value around us. For Murdoch, making the right choices is only possible if we're able to gain a better grip on the forces affecting our inner vision that hinder us from seeing other people correctly.

Murdoch's central parable here is that of a mother, M, who feels towards her daughter-in-law, D, a certain hostility, finding her to be somewhat vulgar, tiresomely juvenile and a poor match for her son. Nevertheless, M behaves properly towards D all the while, such that her real opinion is not discernible from any aspect of her external behaviour. Being both well-intentioned and self-aware of her potential moral faults (e.g. snobbishness, jealousy, prejudice, tendencies to control), M sets herself the task of altering how she sees D. Despite generating no change in her overt actions (given Murdoch's stipulation in this case), we want to say that M's adjustment of her inner vision constitutes morally significant (though unobservable) activity – some inner moral progress. Yet, frustratingly for her, this thing which Murdoch thinks we're 'irresistibly impelled to say' was blocked within the choice-is-all approach to morality.

Murdoch's alternative was influenced heavily by her reading of Simone Weil, the twentieth-century French philosopher, political activist and mystic. In the same year as 'Vision and Choice in Morality', Murdoch also published her review of *The Notebooks of Simone Weil* (trans. Arthur Wills, 1956) for *The Spectator*. This was a pivotal moment in Iris Murdoch's development and career as a moral philosopher; but it also resulted in her withdrawing from the philosophical mainstream. 'Vision and Choice in Morality' was her last paper to be published in the 'standard annals of academic philosophy' in large part, Justin Broackes claims, due to the difficulties associated with 'domesticating within the existing philosophical world the new ideas she was developing from Weil.' Within Weil's Christian Platonist thinking, Murdoch found resources that inspired her re-reading of Plato, which then became the foundation for her own (non-religious) arguments in *The Sovereignty of Good*. The main components of this were: (i) that Good is a transcendent reality, and thus the good person is one who sees things as they are; (ii) that directing our attention to the Good excites love in us; and (iii) that perfection in this regard would result in us no longer having to make choices, since our attention to the reality around us would automatically issue in appropriate action.

Attention becomes a central moral concept; for Murdoch because it captured 'the idea of a just and loving gaze directed upon an individual reality', which she takes to be 'the characteristic and proper mark of the active moral agent'. And, in her view, this is the important effect of changing how we understand moral freedom, as she writes in *The Sovereignty of Good*:

> If we ignore the prior work of attention and notice only the emptiness of the moment of choice we are likely to identify freedom with the outward movement since there is nothing else to identify it with. But if we consider what the work of

attention is like, how continuously it goes on, and how imperceptibly it builds up structures of value round about us, we shall not be surprised that at crucial moments of choice most of the business of choosing is already over.

This issued a serious challenge to modern moral philosophy and laid the foundation for other philosophers (such as Philippa Foot, Elizabeth Anscombe, John McDowell and Bernard Williams) to develop an approach to moral philosophy able to attend to the texture of our inner worlds, and the patterns of character that they produce over the course of our lives. What's interesting, though, is that many of those now working in the area of moral psychology and the related movements in virtue theory, particularism, emotion and moral perception are often completely unaware of Murdoch's role in setting these sites of inquiry in motion. According to Justin Broackes, this influence can be traced principally through McDowell, who gave her complex ideas 'a new frame and support, in a [more domesticable] philosophical context of his own, and showed in sustained and visible debate their power in the philosophical market-place.'

Given Murdoch's prescient philosophic imagination and vision, it is somewhat strange, and unfortunate I think, that her writings lack any real interest in the social and political determinants of what and how we 'see'. There is a growing area of research examining the complex relations between individual virtue and the social world. This has developed partly in response to important findings in psychology relating to, for instance, implicit biases that play a role in racist and sexist judgements and actions. Such cases provide a problem for Murdoch's account, because attending to them at the individual level has been shown to be not only largely ineffectual, but also sometimes detrimental.

We also need, then, to consider the kinds of social and political changes that may be required to support the inner moral work that Murdoch prizes.

Returning to Murdoch as both novelist and philosopher, we can see that this rather anomalous positioning follows somewhat naturally from her philosophic vision. Murdoch's understanding of the relation between moral philosophy and narrative fiction was outlined in a number of interviews, particularly the interviews with Frank Kermode in 1965 (part of the BBC's Modern Novelists series) and Bryan Magee in 1977 (part of the BBC's Modern Philosophy series ironically titled 'Men of Ideas') – both of which are easily accessible and worth watching. In the former she states that, 'Philosophy is very different stuff from fiction; writing philosophy is a very different job [since] one's aiming at a different result . . . But the subject matter is the same, that is, human nature, operating.' Thus, the layered textures of experience that she sought to record and explore in her novels are, according to Martha Nussbaum, 'the stuff of philosophy as well as the stuff of life'. Both in art and in morals, one seeks the discovery of reality.

Murdoch was happily (though not always faithfully) married to John Bayley – a literary critic, writer and professor of English at Oxford University – from 1956 until her death in February 1999, at the age of seventy-nine. Bayley wrote *Elegy for Iris* (1999), which lovingly told the story of their relationship and of her fight with Alzheimer's disease. It was a very great tragedy that someone so invested in discovering reality would have her own slip away; that someone so skilled with language and so rare a thinker would suffer the loss of these faculties. The memoir provided the basis for the film *Iris* (dir. Richard Eyre, 2001), in which Murdoch is portrayed by Kate Winslet and Judi Dench.

Iris Murdoch's deep influence on moral philosophy has not always been adequately recognised, though thankfully this is now changing. Despite her retreat from academic philosophy, philosophers today are increasingly returning to and being inspired by Murdoch's work. I look forward to seeing the further influence that Iris Murdoch and her work might have on the future of moral and political philosophy.

Mary Midgley

1919–2018

Ellie Robson

Mary Midgley was a vibrant moral philosopher whose inexhaustible imagination and persistent questioning of the twentieth-century analytic philosophical paradigm spanned her long life. But despite her refreshingly accessible style of writing and engagement with real-world problems, Midgley's broader philosophical vision has been largely unappreciated. Certain aspects of her work are widely known – such as her engagement with animal ethics and criticism of Richard Dawkins – but the breadth of Midgley's philosophy stretches far beyond these topics.

Unlike many other analytic moral philosophers who often focus on abstract puzzles or defend specific philosophical doctrines, Midgley was more concerned with broadening and augmenting our vision of things. Her books brim with rich ideas about human moral life, particularly examining human beings, our nature, and our place within the world. Yet once you read Midgley's books you will notice similar themes and messages – in this sense, Midgley's philosophy may be described as both holistic and systematic. Engaging in debates of modern science, evolution, environmental ethics and feminism, her philosophy displays a constant and pragmatic concern for the next 'task at hand'. She presents a positive and problem-solving approach to the everyday anxieties we face in our modern world.

Midgley wasn't always sure about her philosophical direction. Her academic career took a somewhat unusual shape. Whereas most of her contemporaries published a steady stream of books and articles, Midgley focused on being a teacher, scholar and mother, only writing academic philosophy towards the end of her professional career. This unlikelier path may have slowed the uptake of Midgley's philosophy into the philosophical literature but, as Midgley tells us in her ever-sensible tone, she was 'jolly glad' she waited until her fifties to publish: 'I didn't know what I thought before then!'

Midgley's memoir, *The Owl of Minerva* (2005), presents a thoughtful and light-hearted portrayal of her early life. Born in London in 1919, Mary was the daughter of politically minded parents, Lesley and Tom Scrutton. Her father later became a chaplain at King's College, Cambridge. In 1924 the Scruttons moved to Greenford, Middlesex, where Mary enjoyed a typically middle-class upbringing. She describes her nature-loving childhood, recalling timeless outdoor adventures with her brother, Hugh. Aged twelve, she began attending Downe House, a girls' boarding school near Newbury. Immersed in poetry, Latin and drama, she recalls reading Plato at sixteen and thinking it was 'tremendous stuff'.

In 1938, Midgley began reading Mods and Greats at Somerville College, Oxford. Among the minority of women philosophy students, she describes entering Oxford at a time when philosophy was dominated by clever young men. Philosophy, to these men, was a competition to win arguments in fractious displays of intelligence – the aim was not advancing understanding but avoiding appearing weak. A. J. Ayer's *Language, Truth and Logic* had appeared only two years earlier and was highly influential. In it, Ayer argues for a trenchant separation of fact and value. But this left ethical questions within an autonomous sphere, devoid of any factual content. It also reduced the work of the moral philosopher to little more than linguistic analysis.

Midgley was not satisfied with this 'moral philosophy' that Oxford offered her and luckily, she was not alone. At Oxford she befriended three like-minded philosophers – Elizabeth Anscombe, Philippa Foot and Iris Murdoch – all of whom went on to be formidable philosophers in their own right. When the war began in 1939, many young men were enlisted, leaving this quartet in a unique historical position – freed from the prevailing demographic norms of male-dominated study. Midgley and her friends would use their wartime education, taught by older dons and conscientious objectors, to offer an alternative moral philosophy to the Ayer-inspired paradigms that had taken Oxford by storm. Instead of engaging in relentless linguistic analysis, these women again focused on placing ethics back into the sphere of human experience. The legacy of their collective work is still being charted by the In Parenthesis project at Durham University, led by Clare Mac Cumhaill and Rachael Wiseman.

In 1950, Mary married fellow philosopher Geoff Midgley and the couple moved to Newcastle, where they spent their entire professional lives. After raising her three sons, Midgley began to write. Despite her late start, once Mary began to publish there was no stopping her: between the ages of fifty-nine and ninety-nine she wrote over two hundred books, articles and chapters, contributing frequently to *New Scientist* and the

Guardian. Her energetic tone and straightforward good sense continued to sound through radio broadcasts, and for many years she spoke on programmes such as Radio 4's *The Moral Maze* and *Woman's Hour.* She engaged directly with notable thinkers of the day, such as Richard Dawkins and Daniel Dennett, and became a renowned moral philosopher and public intellectual. Midgley published her last book, *What Is Philosophy For?*, in 2018, just before her death at the age of ninety-nine.

Midgley's thought is holistic, which makes it difficult to place in any particular philosophical 'box'. Unlike the linguistic paradigm dominant in the Oxford of her youth, according to Midgley there is no significant distance between philosophy and human life; to pass from one to the other is much like walking around the rooms of a house – effortless and familiar. 'Philosophy,' she writes in *The Owl of Minerva*, 'is not a luxury but a necessity' – it is an inevitable part of the human condition, much like growing up or falling in love. When we do philosophy, we should not operate as 'isolated intellectuals', taking part in a sterile enterprise – rather we are part of a collaborative, living process of shared human development. Philosophy is simply and naturally human. As a human endeavour, Midgley's conception of philosophy rejects the distinctions between fact and value, a practice so prominent among Midgley's male contemporaries.

Midgley's conception of philosophy as oriented around real-world problems is most visible in her meta-philosophy – that is, her view on the approach and role of the moral philosopher. Detailed in *Utopias, Dolphins and Computers: Problems of Philosophical Plumbing* (1996), Midgley's enduring comparison is between philosophy and plumbing. Both concern underlying structures that play a vital yet unnoticed role in supplying people with necessary resources for everyday life, quietly working below the surface of our attention, exposed only when they break down in floods of confusion. When this happens, and our concepts become stagnant, it is the job of the philosopher, like the plumber, to 'pull up the floorboards' and examine our faulty concepts, setting about trying to fix the problem.

This powerful metaphor underlines Midgley's argument for the centrality of philosophy to life. Philosophy really does matter. Even if, like the plumbing, we can get away with ignoring it for a long time, sooner or later the myths which we live our lives by – to borrow a turn of phrase from Midgley – will become stagnant and need repairing.

One constant theme of Midgley's philosophy is that of 'world-pictures' or 'myths' – imaginative visions, expressing stories about the kind of norms and practices human society lives by. In *The Myths We Live By* (2003), Midgley unsettles many of these – for instance, the myth of the social contract is still prevalent today. Popularised by Enlightenment philosophy, this is the idea that 'morality is essentially just a contract', freely entered into by isolated and autonomous individuals within a society. In her autobiography Midgley notes that the practice of unsettling myths demonstrates to what extent philosophy is like therapy; an essential activity 'when things become dark and difficult to see, rather than when they are clear and straightforward'. But while she recognises that such broad visions are needed, she thinks problems arise when we are tempted to think that one story or vision can capture the world in all its complexity; our vision is then prone to being one-sided and reductive. She does not argue that the social contract myth is false, but rather that it is a 'typical piece of Enlightenment simplification'.

This notion of embracing the multi-faceted complexity of 'this deeply puzzling world' places Midgley at odds with an increasing philosophical tendency to reduce and level out the moral scene. That is, the tendency to fixate upon some singular idea or entity – genes, competition, markets – so as to give a unified explanation of moral reality. Midgley airs her suspicions of this tendency by criticising notions such as 'social atomism' and the 'selfish gene' in *Science as Salvation* (1992) and *The Solitary Self* (2010). In a similar vein, she warns us of the dangers of 'exaggerated individualism' encouraged by an unrealistic acceptance of a radically competitive human nature in modern versions of Victorian social Darwinism. In *Evolution as a Religion* (1985) she suggests that modern scientific figures such as Richard Dawkins have distorted Darwin's theory of evolution to create the harmful myth that human beings are radically isolated individuals, homeless in a natural world that is an arena of relentless competition. This is a damaging myth for Midgley, because it encourages us to see ourselves as 'disembodied minds' rather than 'earthly creatures' – a self-conception that will likely lead to our lives going badly. Again, Midgley is drawn back to this idea that philosophy is not a solitary endeavour. Rather, our philosophy, like our plumbing, is a shared cooperative and collaborative exercise needed to 'keep the water flowing', and to co-construct pictures that we live by.

So, what is Midgley's vision of ethics? According to *Beast and Man* (1978), philosophy is the study of our complex nature and our situation within the natural world. It is a study of very real bonds of friendship, kinship and social dependence, and of how we live as dependent social beings. Her moral philosophy, then, may be broadly placed within the camp of ethical naturalism, the idea that ethics is dependent on facts of human life, facts that must be discovered by careful study of the human animal. Our rich culture is therefore embedded in and enabled by the natural world, rather than alien to it. However, Midgley's naturalism is not reductive. Much like the naturalism present in Philippa Foot's *Natural Goodness* (2001) Midgley suggests our ethical and rational natures are a rich and complex product of our human 'life form'.

Midgley's consistent emphasis on dependence, relationships and holism are highly relevant to contemporary philosophical debates in feminism, environmental ethics and animal ethics. In *Beast and Man*, Midgley describes another problematic myth, namely the misconception that there is some great division between humans and animals – between the lawless mechanistic 'beast', and the rational, intelligent 'man'. For Midgley, we can learn very little about our true nature by drawing this harsh distinction – especially when we become trapped in this narrow tool of dualism. Instead, we must situate ourselves among the animals; 'We are not just rather like animals; we *are* animals.' Midgley's naturalism encourages us to view the human animal as equally responsive to instincts as the rest of the animal kingdom. Again, we find a common thread in Midgley's writing, a criticism of this fantastical notion of isolated man, espoused by the myth of the isolated individual.

Encouraging philosophers to reinterpret the myth of Beast and Man offers fruitful perspectives on our treatment of non-human animals, and our relationship with the natural environment more broadly. Seeing ourselves as continuous with the natural world reframes discussion about human practices – such as the meat industry – that damage the planet we live in.

So what is Midgley's legacy? Underpinning Midgley's prolific writing is a myth of her own. A picture of a philosophical human being, who is at the same time an animal. A being who lives in accordance with 'world-pictures' yet nonetheless refuses the urge to reduce and simplify in the ever-changing world. For Midgley, embracing this myth involves painting over the shallow myth of the isolated man, and drawing in its place a richer, multifaceted picture of a human animal at home in the natural world. As a philosopher Midgley was truly ahead of her time. I sincerely encourage you to pick up her philosophy.

Elizabeth Anscombe

1919–2001

Hannah Carnegy-Arbuthnott

Elizabeth Anscombe is one of the most important figures of twentieth-century philosophy and one of its most interesting characters. Born in Ireland in 1919, and later schooled in South London, Anscombe won a scholarship to St Hugh's College, Oxford, to study classics and philosophy, or Mods and Greats as it was known. She was so brilliant at philosophy that she achieved a first class degree, despite a dismal performance in the ancient history exams. (Roger Teichmann tells us she ended her oral exam by answering 'no' to the following questions: 'Can you give us the name of a Roman provincial governor?' and (in some desperation) 'Is there any fact about the period you are supposed to have studied which you would like to tell us?') So started an illustrious career which was to span several decades, produce seminal contributions to philosophy, and profoundly influence her students, many of whom would also become well-known philosophers. Alongside her professional achievements, Anscombe, a devout Catholic, raised seven children with her husband and fellow philosopher Peter Geach. As her colleague Philippa Foot remarked, these achievements could only have been possible for a woman of 'monumental strength of mind, will and body'.

Anscombe published important works in metaphysics, history of philosophy, philosophy of mind, moral philosophy and philosophy of religion. Her best-known book, *Intention* (1957), is widely hailed as a classic of modern philosophy, and has been described as the defining moment in twentieth-century philosophy of action. Likewise, her article 'Modern Moral Philosophy' (1958) stimulated the contemporary development of virtue ethics. But it was as a translator that Anscombe first found recognition, publishing the authoritative English version of Wittgenstein's *Philosophical Investigations* in 1953.

Anscombe met Wittgenstein at Newnham College, Cambridge, as a graduate research student. She attended Wittgenstein's lectures, becoming one of his most devoted students and, eventually, a close friend. When Wittgenstein died, Anscombe was one of three literary executors named in his will. She edited and co-edited several volumes of Wittgenstein's posthumous works, produced translations of many of his texts, and wrote *An Introduction to Wittgenstein's Tractatus* (1959). After her graduate studies, Anscombe became a fellow at Somerville College, Oxford, before finally returning in the latter stage of her career to take up Wittgenstein's chair in philosophy at Cambridge. However, while Wittgenstein undoubtedly influenced her work, their relationship was certainly not one of discipleship. Anscombe's body of work spans far beyond the commentaries she published on Wittgenstein's work. Moreover, while Wittgenstein was sceptical of the very existence of ethical propositions, much of Anscombe's philosophy tackled first-order moral questions head on. Despite disagreeing in their attitudes and approaches to moral philosophy and to practical political problems, part of what endeared Anscombe to Wittgenstein was her staunch independence of thought.

Anscombe's independence is evident across her work, and not only in its originality. She was not the kind of philosopher to develop a particular theoretical system and then apply it to various topics. Instead, she was, as Teichmann puts it, 'infuriatingly prone to take each case on its merits.' Much of her work was prompted by a dissatisfaction with existing approaches to some field, and a drive to address important underlying questions which had been overlooked or neglected. The philosophers that Anscombe most respected were not necessarily those who she thought came to the right conclusions, but the ones whose work got at deep and important problems. In 'Modern Moral Philosophy', she remarks about Hume that he was a mere sophist – albeit a brilliant one – but that in noticing his sophistry, one notices matters worthy of further exploration. In her own words, 'The obvious stands in need of investigation as a result of the points that Hume pretends to have made.' This opening up of new topics was something Anscombe prized most highly, and enough to make Hume in her eyes a 'very profound and great philosopher, despite his sophistry.'

While Anscombe's work often defies categorisation, her philosophy is characterised by its overarching ambition to fully address fundamental questions about our psychological and moral nature. And in order to solve these philosophical puzzles, she thought it useful to analyse ordinary concepts, how we learn and acquire them, and to consider what concepts we might have had if we were different kinds of beings altogether.

Her groundbreaking work *Intention* addresses the nature of agency through an investigation of the difference between intentions, predictions, motives and causes. Anscombe wrote

Intention after being perplexed by supporters of the US President Harry Truman, who had made the decision to drop the atomic bomb on the Japanese cities of Hiroshima and Nagasaki in August 1945. Anscombe had opposed the decision of Oxford University to award Truman an honorary degree, on the grounds that this attack was morally abhorrent. However, Truman had received widespread support at the time for what many saw as a difficult decision aimed at ending the Second World War. As John Haldane reports, Anscombe 'came to the conclusion that they had failed to understand the nature of his actions, and it was this that led her to write *Intention*, in which she pointed out that in doing one thing (moving one's hand) one may intentionally be doing another (directing the death of human beings).'

Anscombe argues that we can best understand the differences between kinds of intentional action by considering how actions can be explained and justified. Anscombe drew attention to the importance of action falling 'under a description' with respect to these different concepts. For example, imagine a man who has been hired by a group of people to pump water to their house from a well. As it turns out, the well has been poisoned by some other person who wants the inhabitants of the house to die. In this case, there are several true descriptions of what the man is doing. He is pumping water to the house, earning wages, making a clicking noise with the machine, and causing the deaths of the people inside. But in order to find out his intention, we have to ask the right kind of question – a 'why' question. 'How' questions, on the other hand, won't identify his intention, but might provide answers about ordinary causal conditions, such as that the pump was operated by exerting downward pressure on the handle.

This allows us to determine which descriptions of the action are relevant to assessing the man's intentions. So while it might be true that he is causing the deaths of the people in the house, this is not one of his intentional actions. On the other hand, if he were to find out that the water was poisoned, and to continue to pump it into the house regardless, it would be appropriate to say that poisoning the inhabitants was an intentional action of his, even if he did not directly desire to harm them. The man is acting intentionally in that he intends to pump the poisoned water into the house, and poisoning the inhabitants is a foreseen consequence of that action. However, some causal consequences of actions are to be distinguished from intentional action, such as when my intentional action of cooking meatballs for dinner causes my dog to come into the kitchen.

Anscombe's interest in understanding the nature of intention was closely connected to its role in our moral assessments of what we do. Anscombe took aim at the way contemporary moral philosophers had treated intentions in quite excoriating fashion in 'Modern Moral Philosophy'. She criticises Henry Sidgwick, the Victorian moral philosopher, for arguing that a person should be taken to intend any foreseen consequence of voluntary action. This view of intention informed Sidgwick's ethical thesis that a person is responsible for any and all foreseen consequences of her voluntary action, whether or not she desired those consequences. Anscombe thought it 'quite characteristic of very bad degenerations of thought on such questions' that Sidgwick's thesis sounded quite edifying on the face of it.

Anscombe points out that Sidgwick's thesis leads us to assess the badness or goodness of an action solely by its consequences. However, this leaves people able to make excuses for even the worst actual consequences of their bad actions, by arguing that they did not foresee them. Against Sidgwick, Anscombe contended that 'A man is responsible for the bad consequences of his *bad* actions, but gets no credit for the good ones; and contrariwise is not responsible for the bad consequences of *good* actions.' Part of Sidgwick's mistake, in Anscombe's view, was to deny the distinction between foreseen and intended consequences. Furthermore, she suggested that the intrinsic goodness or badness of certain acts must factor into our assessment of moral responsibility for intentional actions. Anscombe coined the term *consequentialism* to refer to Sidgwick's brand of philosophy. Though she invoked the term rather scathingly, it has since become cemented as a significant branch of moral philosophy in its own right.

Anscombe's wider point in 'Modern Moral Philosophy' held not only against consequentialism but was aimed at all modern approaches to moral philosophy, which relied on the idea of some moral law whose standards we must adhere to. Anscombe argued that the reference to a legalistic structure was a hangover from the days when morality was based on religious law. Without the concept of a divine lawgiver, however, concepts such as right and wrong no longer had meaning. Anscombe held no punches in her criticism of these views, calling Mill's principle of utility 'stupid' and Kant's idea of legislating for oneself 'absurd'. Anscombe suggested that it was futile to continue with moral philosophy until we had an adequate account of human psychology. Specifically, we would need a philosophical basis for understanding what creatures like us need in order to flourish. Knowing what human flourishing consists of would shed light on which actions in which contexts should be considered virtuous. In light of this, 'Modern Moral Philosophy' has been widely interpreted as a plea for a return to virtue ethics, and it certainly paved the way for neo-Aristotelians such as Philippa Foot, Alasdair MacIntyre and Rosalind Hursthouse to bring virtue ethics back to mainstream philosophy.

However, some, such as Roger Crisp, argue that we should read 'Modern Moral Philosophy' as an argument for the superiority of a religious-based ethics. Anscombe was, after all, a devout Catholic, and her religious commitments often found expression in her philosophy. Anscombe first converted to Roman Catholicism after reading various theological texts between the ages of twelve and fifteen. As is often the case with converts, she took her faith incredibly seriously.* It was also thanks to that reading that she became interested in philosophy. She had read two arguments in a nineteenth-century text called *Natural Theology* which she found puzzling. The first was the claim that God knows what anybody would have done if they hadn't died when they did. Anscombe didn't believe that there were any such facts about what would have happened if things had been different to how they actually happened. The second was a 'First Cause' argument for the existence of God, and it was in attempts to improve that argument that Anscombe first began doing philosophy. Her faith and philosophy were again brought together in her later work on 'Contraception and Chastity' (1972), where she again invoked the idea of actions being intended under a description to make the case that while barrier methods of contraception are forbidden by Catholic doctrine, there is no such problem with the rhythm method. That article courted controversy for some comments that Anscombe made in it regarding abortion and sodomy. Michael Tanner and Bernard Williams accused her of accepting rotten thinking from the Pope and the

---

* According to a priest with whom she used to take Mass, Anscombe would sometimes lie flat on her stomach, arms outstretched, during the consecration of the Eucharist. Thinking she had fallen down, people would try to help her up, and she would just shake them off.

Church. Anscombe responded, wryly addressing her reply to 'my friendly neighbourhood philosophers'.

Anscombe certainly took philosophical argumentation very seriously, whether she was engaging with famous philosophers, archbishops or undergraduate students (she once wrote to the Archbishop of Armagh to point out a mistake he had made in a piece about Wittgenstein's *Tractatus*). Michael Dummett, who was a student of Anscombe, remarked that she would attack most vigorously any arguments with which he thought she would agree, sometimes stretching the tutorial well over its allotted time. Taking an argument seriously was a way of showing respect to her interlocutor regardless of their status.

As a woman in the male-dominated world of Oxbridge philosophy, this could sometimes cause friction. Anscombe's first journal publication was a critique of a chapter of C. S. Lewis's book *Miracles* (1947). She read this paper at a meeting of the Oxford Socratic Club, where Lewis himself was present. Some reported that the meeting was the most dramatic in the club's history, as Anscombe had launched a heavy attack on Lewis and left him deeply disturbed and quite horrified. Anscombe's own recollection was that 'it was an occasion of sober discussion of certain quite definite criticisms' and remarked that 'some of his friends seem not to have been interested in the actual arguments or the subject matter.' Reading these conflicting accounts, one can't help but wonder whether it was actually the presence of a woman directing an intelligent argument against a well-known author that caused such shock among the gentlemen present.

Anscombe certainly faced reminders that she was a woman in a man's world. When she walked into a proctor's office at Cambridge on her first day taking over Wittgenstein's chair of philosophy, Anscombe wore her usual trousers and tabard. She was greeted by one of the clerks, who asked if she was the new cleaning lady. Her habit of wearing trousers didn't go down too well with the dress code regulators at Cambridge, either, who told her that women had to wear skirts while lecturing. Anscombe would therefore reportedly come to lectures with a skirt in a plastic bag and pull it on over her trousers. On another occasion, legend has it that when an upscale restaurant in Boston told her that they didn't admit women in trousers, she simply took them off.

Anscombe was a formidable woman if there ever was one, and, in many ways, the quintessential philosopher. There isn't space here to tell you about all aspects of her impressively wide-ranging body of work, but I highly recommend you take the time to read some first-hand. It is always witty, challenging and rewarding in equal measure.

Mary Warnock

1924–2019

Gulzaar Barn

Although the aim of this collection has been to showcase women philosophers who have typically been neglected from the canon, one of the first books of philosophy that I happened to read was by a philosopher who was a woman. The book was *An Intelligent Person's Guide to Ethics* (1998) by Mary Warnock, given to me by my parents when I was in my final year of sixth form, after I had decided I wanted to study philosophy at university. Unfortunately the book allowed me to formulate the rather false impression that philosophy was always this digestible and lucid. I then most notably came into contact with Warnock's work during my postgraduate studies when I was writing on the ethical concerns raised by the practice of commercial surrogacy. Here, I learned that Warnock had chaired the Committee of Inquiry into Human Fertilisation and Embryology (1984), which directly influenced the Surrogacy Arrangements Act (1985). I was awestruck that a philosopher had been appointed to such an important role and had exerted such an impact on policy. It was her application of philosophy to the public realm which Warnock embodies that really resonated with me and inspired the writing of this chapter.

Warnock was born in 1924 in Winchester, the youngest child of seven. Her father, who had taught modern languages at Winchester College, died seven months before her birth. Despite this tragedy, Warnock describes herself in her memoir as having a 'supremely happy childhood'. Warnock, to all intents and purposes, had a rather privileged upbringing: meals were brought upstairs to her by a maid, she and her siblings had a nanny, to whom she formed a deep attachment, and she attended public day and boarding schools. Amusingly, Warnock recalls that, aged fifteen, she knew she was a 'natural Tory': 'I loved hunting; I loved time-honoured hierarchies; I loved cathedrals.' However, as the Second World War unfolded around her, Warnock felt that to indulge these 'Trollopian instincts' would be wrong. She decided to 'check her privilege', as is encouraged now, and became 'woke' – 'I must pull myself together, recognise the unfairness of my privilege and comfortable way of life, begin properly to aim for a classless society, think about politics, become someone who would go to what I vaguely thought of as meetings. By 1945, I had talked myself pretty thoroughly round to the left.' Conversion techniques that would put modern political campaigns to shame! Warnock adds that her husband, Geoffrey Warnock – fellow and tutor in philosophy at Magdalen College, principal of Hertford College, and later vice-chancellor of the University of Oxford – was much more wholeheartedly of the left than she was, and was instrumental in finalising her change in political direction.

Warnock's life at Oxford seemed dizzyingly glamorous and enviable. She won a scholarship to read Mods and Greats – an undergraduate degree focusing on ancient Greek and Latin literature, history and philosophy – at Lady Margaret Hall.

Warnock says she would not have won this scholarship had she not attended Prior's Field School, in Surrey, which had greatly improved her self-confidence. The school, founded by the Huxley family, and attended by both Aldous and Julian, paid great attention to politics and culture. Being an undergraduate during the war, however, was not all that enjoyable. Wartime regulations meant that Mods and Greats, normally a four-year course, had to be shortened. Warnock's studies were further disrupted by the war, and she left to teach at Sherborne School for Girls for two years, until Lady Margaret Hall would have her back. After finishing her undergraduate degree, Warnock rushed to complete the then newly instated postgraduate B.Phil. in philosophy within one year, rather than the customary two (apologies if you have experienced the B.Phil and this thought creates pangs of anxiety). Following this, Warnock was elected to a lectureship at St Hugh's College, and her husband Geoffrey was elected to a prize fellowship at Magdalen College.

Philosophy at Oxford during the period Warnock taught there was at a 'high pitch of success'. The B.Phil. was attracting graduates from all over the world, and figures such as Philippa Foot, Gilbert Ryle and J. L. Austin were roaming the cloisters. Warnock and her husband were hobnobbing with figures such as Isaiah Berlin, Peter and Ann Strawson, and having Kingsley and Hilary Amis to stay. As principal of Hertford College, Geoffrey Warnock even had his portrait painted by David Hockney. Warnock recalls how, during this period, the Oxford left-wing dons had links with the Labour Party and would advise on policy. Indeed, 'it was among these people that the Common Market as a first tentative adumbration was tentatively discussed.'

Warnock also met Margaret Thatcher a number of times. Warnock talks at length in her memoir about Thatcherism and laments the dismantling of higher education through cuts to university grants, and through the new onus placed on universities to satisfy the requirements of industry. Crucially, Warnock ventures, the most pervasive legacy of Thatcher's was the 'assumption that nothing matters except the non-squandering of money, and that no value exists except to save and prosper.' As well as believing this in relation to the state, individuals began adopting this value for themselves.

Increasingly, people talked about 'offers they could not refuse'. And these, of course, were offers they could have refused, but did not want to, because they were offers that would enrich them. In such a culture it becomes increasingly easy to cross the line between honest and dishonest means of becoming rich. If personal wealth is generally seen as the highest value, then the means to attain it may gradually become a matter of indifference. The erosion of moral standards in the City and the stock market illustrates what may come to seem inevitable.

Warnock demonstrated a clear commitment to values outside of and beyond enrichment, for example in her committee's distinctly anti-marketisation stance on surrogacy in 1984. Negotiating surrogacy on a commercial basis is illegal in the UK under the Surrogacy Arrangements Act (1985). The inquiry led by Warnock concluded that the danger of exploitation outweighed the potential benefits of commercial surrogacy. It stated that treating people as means to one's own ends becomes 'positively exploitative when financial interests are involved.' It would seem that Warnock et al. deemed surrogacy to fall outside the proper scope of the market, the use of surrogates by companies perhaps constituting a dishonest means of becoming rich.

While it may be the case that commercial surrogacy is prohibited here in the UK, it has flourished elsewhere. India has emerged as a 'leader' of commercial surrogacy, with the Confederation of Indian Industry predicting the industry now generates US$2.3 billion annually. The Indian surrogacy industry is characterised by wealthy international clients procuring the services of Indian surrogates who are comparatively and absolutely less well off. Much of the philosophical scholarship in the area points to the exploitative nature of Indian surrogacy arrangements. Theorists such as Vida Panitch and Stephen Wilkinson fall shy of advocating prohibitive intervention, however, arguing that exploitative surrogacy often serves as a best possible option for disadvantaged women under non-ideal constraints. In recent years, the Indian government's position on surrogacy has dramatically shifted, coinciding with the increased scholarship in this area, suggesting the possible influence of academic and media attention. The lower house of the Indian parliament passed the Surrogacy (Regulation) Bill in December 2018, effectively prohibiting commercial surrogacy, replacing it with a locally regulated altruistic model, available to Indian nationals only.

The UK's own surrogacy laws are also currently under a three-year review by the Law Commission of England and Wales, and that of Scotland. One key area targeted for reform is the way in which uncertainty in the law may be encouraging UK residents to look overseas for surrogates. Warnock has rather candidly since admitted that she believes she had an 'irrational prejudice' against permitting surrogacy, and that she followed her gut feelings, 'quite illegitimately'. The prohibition of surrogacy on commercial grounds has arguably had a bearing on the emergence of industries elsewhere to cater for demand: it is reported that Britons are the largest consumers of the industry in India. The act of liberalising surrogacy laws in the UK may serve to redistribute some of the existing harms presented by the issue, in terms of reducing the burden on surrogates in other countries to fulfil demand. However, a parallel problem of exploitation may persist if surrogates from the UK are also typically contracting out of socioeconomic vulnerability, albeit to a lesser degree.

Warnock has been credited with promoting the discipline of 'bioethics' as a vital intermediary between politics, the public and biomedicine. Bioethics is often understood as the study of issues arising from advances in biology, medicine and healthcare. Issues considered under this banner typically include abortion, euthanasia, clinical research ethics and the allocation of scarce healthcare resources. It has been suggested by Duncan Wilson that the development of bioethics and 'ethics committees' like the ones Warnock has been involved with 'tallied with the Conservative government's desire for increased surveillance of hitherto autonomous professions'. Nevertheless, Wilson argues that this political demand 'fulfilled Warnock's belief that philosophers should apply themselves to practical matters. And once selected as chair of the government inquiry, she became a strong advocate of what became known as "bioethics": criticising biomedical paternalism and extolling the benefits of external oversight.'

In her memoir, Warnock describes the difficulties involved in putting together the final report of the committee on human fertilisation and embryology. She recalls that it was hard to reach agreement and encourage members to state clearly what their objections were, after they had indicated that 'they "were not happy" about this or that'. Warnock also suggests that the solution to such irreconcilable differences did not quite lie in aiming for a 'correct' answer, but rather, included proposing 'something practical, regretted no doubt by some as too lax, by others as too strict, but something to which, whatever their reservations, everyone would be prepared to consent.'

This desire to 'reach a consensus' in the face of such obstructing plurality is echoed in the introduction to Warnock's book *An Intelligent Person's Guide to Ethics*, where she laments the effect that logical positivism had on moral and political philosophy. Logical positivism was a movement that emerged within philosophy in the 1920s. It held that there were only two meaningful types of propositions: those that were necessarily and objectively true, such as mathematical propositions, and propositions that were rendered facts through verification by observable evidence, such as facts emerging from empirical scientific study. This approach had the effect of rendering value judgements in moral philosophy, such as 'this action is good/right/wrong', as meaningless. Such statements, after all, could not be verified or falsified in this way. Warnock took issue with this denigration of the notion of subjective 'value' in favour of objective 'fact', believing that questions must be asked 'about values, what we value and why, and who "we" are when we are inclined to raise these problems.'

Relatedly, Warnock was also perturbed by moral relativism, the doctrine that the truth or justification of moral judgments is not absolute but is relative to the moral standard of some person or group of persons. Such a view holds that there exist deep and widespread moral disagreements, and there is no universal set of moral principles that can adjudicate between them. For Warnock, however, 'altruism, or unselfishness' is central to morality. Goodness is not merely in the eye of the beholder. Rather, 'there are shared and permanent values, arising from the nature of humanity itself.' Decisions must aim towards some civic and social good. This relates to the root of Warnock's disagreement with Thatcherism – that the selfishness it encouraged served to undermine the idea of a common good. Crucially, such Thatcherite selfishness is 'hard to reconcile with the qualities of a truly civilised society.' At her core, therefore, Warnock might be read as a communitarian, primarily concerned with the role of the individual in relation to a social community, with actions that further the stability and cohesion of the whole seen as constituting the good.

Warnock describes the book *The Spirit of Man* (1916), an anthology containing Shakespeare's sonnets, other poems, and extracts from Spinoza, Tolstoy and Plato, as 'undoubtedly the most educative book' she ever possessed. She was a great believer in the power of stories to encapsulate values that are 'permanent, intelligible, and above all shared.' It is clear that Warnock thoroughly enjoyed, and was deeply grateful for, her own school and university education. This appreciation seems to be reflected in her belief that significant value lies in educating children about ethics, as well as cultivating their imagination. Warnock was able to further these sentiments through her role in the 1978 Committee of Enquiry into the Education of Handicapped Children and Young People, which laid the foundations for reform in special needs education. This enquiry encouraged, in particular, social acceptance, and served to change the way we thought about disability, by challenging unhelpful labels and dogmas. Crucially, Warnock emphasised the value of education for all, seeing it as a 'road down which every child had to walk', reiterating the idea of a common good, towards which education must aim.

Warnock has been highly successful in bridging dialogue between the academy, parliament and the scientific community. She has been able to do this while remaining steadfast in a commitment to questioning what society ought to value, and exploring how seemingly divergent areas of inquiry can be united in the pursuit of the civic good.

Sophie Bosede Oluwole

1935–2018

Minna Salami

To consider the life and work of Sophie Bosede Oluwole, the erudite and provocative shaper of contemporary Yoruba classical philosophy, we must start with a brief history of the Yoruba people of today's Nigeria. It is this history that underpins the foundations of her philosophical work.

Most importantly, to understand Oluwole's position, we should be aware that there was no such thing as Nigeria only as recently as the early twentieth century. Yorubas were instead part of the Oyo Empire, which stretched across modern day southwestern Nigeria to Benin and Togo. The Oyo Empire consisted of numerous city-states which it had conquered. One of those was Ondo State, where Professor Oluwole was born in 1935.

By the time of Oluwole's birth, Nigeria had been a British colony for twenty-one years. In 1914, the last of the Yoruba city-states (the Egba kingdom) had been abolished and the entire Oyo Empire, along with caliphates and kingdoms to the north and east of the River Niger – whose fluvial mysteries had been the initial motive for British exploration in the region – were amalgamated into one big colony: Nigeria.

To what extent did colonisation impact the childhood of a girl born in Ondo State twenty-one years after the formation of Nigeria? Did she consider herself Nigerian first, or Yoruba first? To what extent was the colonisation of the mind in effect in those relatively early days of British rule? Perhaps the story about how she came to be called Sophie gives us an indication. Until Oluwole was eight years old she went by the name Bosede, but because she performed so well in school, her headmaster suggested that her father rename her Sophia, a name he found more appropriate for her because she was so intelligent.

If Anglophone names were seen as a sign of intelligence, then it seems safe to assume that the colonial education had set its mark at this time. For Oluwole's headmaster to suggest that her name be changed, let alone for her family to approve of it, indicates that the colonial mentality must have already been shaping life in Ondo State quite pronouncedly. In fact, Oluwole herself once characteristically said that although she tweaked the name from Sophia to Sophie to personalise it, she kept the name as a testimony to the legacy of colonialism of her people.

Perhaps it was an accident of fate that, if she had to be re-baptised at all, it was at least with a name that forms the field of study – philosophy – to which she would dedicate her life. Philosophy after all comes from 'philo', which means 'love' in Ancient Greek, and 'sophia', which means wisdom; and the love of wisdom was Oluwole's greatest tool.

However, it was a different type of love that led her towards philosophy. In 1963, at twenty-eight years old, Oluwole moved to Moscow with her first husband who had received a scholarship from the USSR. Her first two children (she would have four more) stayed behind with family. She enrolled into university but, once accepted, her husband was transferred to Cologne in West Germany, where Oluwole again applied to study but again missed the opportunity as a year later her husband was transferred to the US. When Oluwole returned to Nigeria from the US in 1967, she finally enrolled at the University of Lagos, where she received both her bachelor's and master's degrees in philosophy. She then moved to the then renowned University of Ibadan, where she was awarded her doctorate in philosophy, the first to be awarded to a Nigerian by a Nigerian university.

By now, Oluwole was beginning to become increasingly conscious of Yoruba thought and African philosophy. Her proposed doctoral thesis was titled 'The Rational Basis of Yoruba Ethical Thinking'. Alas, due to a lack of supervisors on the topic she opted to write a thesis titled 'Meta-ethics and the Golden Rule'. This was another accident of fate perhaps, as her specialisation in the ethics of reciprocation would later – when she indeed did dedicate her oeuvre, in essence, to 'the rational basis of Yoruba thinking' – invigorate her ripostes to accusations of reductionism and fatalism in African philosophy.

Her journey into African philosophy was, as she herself said, 'prompted by my training and experience in Western philosophy.' According to this education, she was taught that 'Africans never originated any cogent tradition of philosophy'. Even at her own doctoral graduation party in 1984, the head of department of philosophy congratulated her for finally attaining 'the license to talk all the nonsense [she] had been talking before.' Oluwole became determined to use her intellectual capacity to prove the sceptics wrong, declaring that she was on a 'crusade to rediscover, revive, criticise, amend and promote indigenous African knowledge'.

By 'crusade' Oluwole referred to lucid criticisms of not only Western philosophers such as Hobbes, Hegel and Rousseau, who blatantly espoused racist views in their writing. She also fearlessly slated leading African philosophers such as Paulin J. Hountondji, Akin Makinde and Kwasi Wiredu, arguing that their claims that scientific civilisations could not exist without writing (Hountondji), that African languages were not complex enough to handle philosophical discourse (Makinde), or that traditional modes of understanding were intuitive and unscientific (Wiredu) were absurd and fictitious. 'It is heretical to identify and/or characterise African thought from definitions derived from Western concepts and traditions of thought,' she argued.

Oluwole contended that African philosophy could be discovered via a hermeneutical approach, the theory or methodology of interpretation, to the oral canon of the continent. With the exception of Ancient Egyptian, Ethiopian and Islamic texts, African epistemology was recorded through proverbs, ritual texts, epic poems, musical traditions, creation myths, life histories, historical narratives and recitations rather than through written works, and it was through studying these sources that philosophical thoughts could be understood.

Through this approach she demonstrated how Yoruba oral genres qualified as philosophy. More specifically, she argued for the interpretation of the 'corpus of Ifá', which is the quintessential Yoruba compendium of philosophical themes such as wisdom, justice, time, human agency, destiny, democracy, misogyny and human rights, as philosophy rather than the system of divination it is commonly assigned. The corpus of Ifá, which now largely also exists in written format, is a geomantic system consisting of 256 figures to which thousands of verses are attached. It has been stored through memory for thousands of years by traditional Yoruba philosophers known as babalawos, which means 'fathers of esoteric knowledge'.

Oluwole's insights and bravado established her as a fearless thinker and soon her classes at the University of Lagos, where she now lectured, filled to the brim. As an unapologetic feminist in an anti-feminist society, her popularity was testimony to her charm and wisdom. Eleven years after her graduation she had already published five books: *Readings in African Philosophy* (1989), *Witchcraft, Reincarnation and the God-Head (Issues in African Philosophy)* (1992), *Womanhood in Yoruba Traditional Thought* (1993), *Democratic Patterns and Paradigms: Nigerian Women's Experience* (1996) and *Philosophy and Oral Tradition* (1997). She was equally prolific in writing papers and editing book volumes.

In her last book, *Socrates and Orunmila: Two Patrons of Classical Philosophy* (2015), Oluwole offered a groundbreaking comparison between Socrates, the founder of Western philosophy, and Orunmila, the creator of the corpus of Ifá. If Socrates could be considered the father of Western philosophy, having left behind no written work of his own, then why shouldn't Orunmila, who is believed to have pre-dated Socrates even, be considered the father of African philosophy? Aside from the parallel that Socrates revolutionised Greek philosophy without writing down his thoughts, and Orunmila's words too were transmitted by his disciples into the oral canon, Oluwole employs a complex and well-researched approach to show how similar their insights were. Where Socrates famously said, 'The unexamined life is not worth living,' Orunmila said, 'The proverb is a conceptual tool of analysis.' Where Plato's Socrates said, 'The highest truth is that which is eternal and unchangeable,' Orunmila said 'Truth is the word that cannot fall.' Where Socrates said, 'God only is wise,'

Orunmila too addressed the limits of human knowledge in his statement that 'no knowledgeable person knows the number of sands'. Oluwole urged western Africa to reclaim its philosophical heritage, contending that the body of knowledge she found in the Yoruba tradition was as rich and complex as any found in the west. As the late German philosopher Professor Heinz Kimmerle writes in a review of the book, 'Oluwole's extensive research into Socrates and Orunmila shows that there are amazing similarities in their life and work.'

Not everyone was equally impressed. As expected, Oluwole's arguments were staunchly opposed by many of her philosopher colleagues. At one conference, a professor commented that Oluwole's claims that the Ifá verses are philosophy were 'embarrassing' and 'nonsensical' (a favourite word of her critics, it seems). But Oluwole, never one to be left speechless, retorted that the corpus of Ifá and the babalawos may, like Socrates, not be philosophers in the narrow sense of academia, such as her colleague and herself, but rather that they are philosophers of the people.

In actual fact, Oluwole was that rare philosopher who was both an academic philosopher and a populist one. I had proof of this when on the morning of 23 December 2018, I closed a Word document containing this very chapter, in progress, and opened my Twitter feed. There it unfathomably was: an announcement of the death of Professor Oluwole, at eighty-three years old. It seemed incomprehensible that someone with the vivacious, sagacious and provocative legacy that I was so intimately engaged with at the time could ever die.

But of course, death offers no debate. And nor, thankfully, does legacy. As the outpourings of commiseration flooded into the Nigerian media, the impact of the philosophical thought

I was writing about became unquestionably clear. Professor Oluwole's output had achieved what good philosophical work truly should do – it had not only produced a vast and pioneering body of academic work, it had challenged the status quo, strived to end ignorance, and offered the general populace an opportunity to rethink what they accept as true.

Angela Davis

b. 1944

Anita L. Allen

Angela Y. Davis was born in Birmingham, Alabama. At the time, African Americans were still segregated on the basis of race by state law and denied basic civil rights enjoyed by whites in the areas of education, housing, public accommodations, police protection and voting. At a time when many Black women in the American South could only aspire to be farm hands or domestics, it would have been impossible to foresee that Angela Davis would grow to become an internationally recognised icon by the age of thirty, and a quintessentially American activist, feminist and academic philosopher.

Davis is perhaps the most iconic symbol of the American Black Power Movement. Exposed to communist and socialist theories by her parents and later as a student, Davis has spent her life working to understand and describe the full extent of capitalist state oppression in the United States, both through her scholarship and her political activism on behalf of Blacks, women, the poor and the powerless. She was a member of the Communist Party for many years, including during the Cold

War with the Soviet Union and the Vietnam War, when the United States defined itself as the enemy of global communism.

Davis first gained nationwide attention in 1969 when the Regents of the University of California attempted to fire her from a teaching position at the University of California Los Angeles (UCLA) for being a communist. Her notoriety grew the following year, when her face wound up on an FBI 'most wanted' fugitive-from-justice poster. She was the subject of a high-profile manhunt that led to her arrest and imprisonment. Guns that Davis had purchased in her name for security purposes were used without her complicity in the siege of a Marin County, California courthouse in which several people were killed. An international campaign called for her release from prison, and Davis was eventually released following acquittal of all criminal charges in a jury trial.

Just as important as her activism surrounding these events and their aftermath, she has also made important scholarly contributions critiquing capitalism by drawing connections between anti-racism, gender equality and prison abolition. The Collegium of Black Women Philosophers honoured Davis at Pennsylvania State University in 2017. A professor emerita from the University of California Santa Cruz, she remains in the national spotlight, as a lightning rod for political controversy. In 2019 her views on Israel and Palestine led to the cancellation of a Birmingham Civil Rights Institute gala at which she was scheduled to receive a human rights award. Davis has advocated boycott, divestment and sanctions against Israel.

The path to philosophical eminence was in Davis's case a rocky road, full of impediments and potential barriers. As an African-American girl growing up in Birmingham, Alabama, in the 1940s and 50s, Angela Davis could easily have set her sights low, undermined by government-backed racist oppression. Yet her parents were bold. In 1948, hers became the first Black family to move into a previously all-white block in town. As more Black families followed hers, the neighbourhood became known as 'Dynamite Hill', reflecting the frequency with which these families had their houses bombed for disrupting the racist hierarchy. Davis would later say the violence she witnessed as a child instilled in her the importance of self-defence and a willingness to fight back against irrational violence.

Davis moved north as a teenager. It was by attending Elisabeth Irwin High School, a private school in New York City known for its radical politics and pedagogy, that Davis was first systematically exposed to socialism, reading the *Communist Manifesto* and getting involved in a communist youth group. Following high school Davis attended Brandeis University on a full scholarship, where she participated in protests and attended visiting lectures by leading thinkers in the struggle for racial justice, such as James Baldwin and Malcolm X. Although Davis majored in French literature, her deepening interest in the philosophy of Karl Marx, and the line of thinkers who influenced and were influenced by him, led her to study philosophy. In her final year at Brandeis she developed a mentorship with the philosopher Herbert Marcuse, who guided her study of philosophy and encouraged her decision to continue in graduate school at the University of Frankfurt, in West Germany.

Davis was comfortable going to Europe for graduate study. She had spent her junior year of college studying in France and spent the summer after her first year of college in Europe as well. While Davis seemed to find her time abroad satisfying, she wrote in her autobiography that, 'The more the struggles at home accelerated, the more frustrated I felt at being forced to experience it all vicariously. I was advancing my studies, deepening my understanding of philosophy, but I felt more and more isolated.' One of the events that contributed to this feeling was the 16th Street Baptist Church bombing in her hometown of Birmingham on Sunday 15 September 1963 that killed four girls who had been her childhood friends: Carole Robertson, Cynthia Wesley, Addie Mae Collins and Carol Denise McNair. Davis learned about the event from the pages of a newspaper while she was in France. She recounted in her autobiography how isolating it was to feel that her white classmates could not appreciate the scope of the violence in Birmingham of which this tragedy was a part.

These experiences of violence from her hometown left a deep impression on Davis. During an interview she gave from prison in 1972, she reflected on the bombings in her neighbourhood, including the one that killed her four friends, as well as memories of Black men leading armed patrols to keep their families safe: 'That's why when someone asks me about violence, I just find it incredible. Because what it means is that the person who is asking that question has absolutely no idea what Black people have gone through, what Black people have experienced in this country, since the time the first Black person was kidnapped from the shores of Africa.'

Davis cut her time in Frankfurt short, and moved to Southern California to continue her graduate studies at the University of California San Diego under her mentor Marcuse, who had relocated there from Brandeis. She earned a master's degree from San Diego. She would eventually earn a PhD in philosophy from the Humboldt University of Berlin. But in the meantime, back in the US, Davis blossomed as a political radical. She had major roles in the Los Angeles chapter of the Student Nonviolent Coordinating Committee (SNCC), a Black Panther Party office in Westside Los Angeles, and a Black Student Union at UC San Diego. Davis became leader, organising many rallies, demonstrations and actions to demand accountability against racial violence and oppression. Davis also led the Los Angeles SNCC's Freedom School, where she and others taught courses on subjects like 'Current Developments in the Black Movement' and 'Community Organising Skills'.

Through her involvement in these political groups, Davis confronted the reality of misogyny and sexism; 'a constant problem in my political life,' she recounted in her autobiography. She was, she has reported, criticised very heavily for doing 'a man's job'. Black women who took initiative and worked to become leaders in their own right threatened men's masculinity. Undeterred, Davis established her undeniable strength as a leader in the movements she was part of, despite these dynamics.

Driven in part by her frustrations with some of the other groups she was involved with, and in part by the appeal communism had long held for her, in July 1968 Davis joined the Che-Lumumba Club, a local Black chapter of the Communist Party USA. That fall, she started a new position teaching philosophy at UCLA, from which she was fired for admitting that she was a communist. When a judge found the university rule prohibiting the hiring of communists unconstitutional, she was reinstated, only to be dismissed later under a different pretext. The university took issue with statements she had made outside of the classroom.

A *New York Times* op-ed on 2 June 1970 excoriated the decision: 'This action will set the Regents, who are doing Governor Reagan's bidding, on a collision course not only with the faculty of the university's campus at Los Angeles but with all defenders of academic freedom.' The national press around the incident made Davis a public figure, and led to a cascade of threats against her life. The publicity also affected her family: her parents lost friends and were ostracised in Birmingham. But Davis did not back down, instead using the attention as an opportunity to challenge the conventional anti-communist narrative that was prevalent at the time. She found that the demonisation of communist philosophy did not take hold as well in non-affluent Black communities in Southern California. 'There must be something good about it,' she recounted one person saying when asking her about communism, 'because the man is always trying to convince us it's bad.'

Davis also used the new platform she found herself with in the midst of the incident to draw attention to other social justice issues about which she was passionate. She played a key role in a defence committee for the Soledad Brothers, three African-American inmates accused of killing a prison guard. Davis used her newfound popularity to speak out about the case – in fact she was leading a rally calling for their release when the final decision to fire her from UCLA was announced.

In August 1970, Jonathan Jackson, the brother of George Jackson (one of the Soledad Brothers), took hostages in a courtroom to free his brother, resulting in the death of a judge, himself and two others. Although she was not there and disavowed any involvement with the crime, the guns legally belonged to Davis, and she was charged with kidnapping and murder under a California provision that would make her just as guilty as Jonathan for the actions of that day. Davis fled, and was eventually captured. Her vocal protestations of innocence and defence of herself attracted a widespread international movement for Angela Davis to be freed. From prison, she wrote about the nature of political prisoners in the United States and published an edited work containing prison critiques from others. Taking its title from a letter from James Baldwin sent to Davis in prison, *If They Come in the Morning: Voices of Resistance* (1971) helped mobilise support for Davis and raise awareness of the injustice of the prison system more broadly. At her trial, Davis was acquitted by an all-white jury.

Following her acquittal, Davis became a professor and continued to speak out on issues of oppression, especially around race, class and gender. Her book *Women, Race and Class* (1981) has become a feminist classic, challenging conventional anti-feminist and feminist narratives alike around Black women (and men). She has continued her advocacy against the 'prison-industrial complex' and is a leading proponent of prison abolition, for which she makes the case in *Are Prisons Obsolete?* (2003). Her speeches on these topics and more broadly on the nature of freedom from oppression are collected in *Women, Culture & Politics* (1989), *The Meaning of Freedom, And Other Difficult Dialogues* (2012) and the most recent *Freedom is a Constant Struggle: Ferguson, Palestine, and the Foundations of a Movement* (2016).

Despite years of peaceful mainstream service in higher education promoting gender, race and prison studies, Davis is no stranger to controversy for her outspoken views. In January 2019, she was in the news for the Birmingham Civil Rights Institute's decision to rescind an invitation to honour her at its annual gala (with an award named after civil rights activist Reverend Fred Shuttlesworth). In a statement, Davis explained that the decision was based on her long-standing support for Palestinian justice. Undeterred, she explained that she would be returning to Birmingham in any case. 'Despite the BCRI's regrettable decision,' she stated, 'I look forward to being in Birmingham in February for an alternative event organised by those who believe that the movement for civil rights in this moment must include a robust discussion of all of the injustices that surround us.' Later that month, the Institute changed course and reissued its invitation.

The number of women of African ancestry who are professional academic philosophers remains small in the United States. Angela Davis was one of the first such women to receive a PhD in philosophy. Joyce Mitchell Cook and Naomi Zack (Zack identifies as mixed-race) also received PhDs in the 1960s. A handful more received PhDs in the 1970s and 1980s. Davis was the only Black woman philosopher I had ever heard of when I read Marcuse, Sartre and Marx in college, and began a PhD programme in philosophy in 1974. In November 2017, soon after I commenced duties as president-elect of the American Philosophical Association Eastern Division, I had the good fortune to meet Davis in person, at the Collegium of Black Women Philosophers' 10th Annual Meeting at which she was honoured. I was not sure what to expect from my first meeting with a person whose beauty, commitment to justice and intelligence have uniquely inspired me since I was sixteen. I found her warm and gracious. She was generous from the podium in publicly acknowledging my far more modest accomplishments. As I watched her address a room full of admirers that included my own college-aged daughter, it was clear that I am not the only one for whom Angela Davis is and will always be a Philosopher Queen.

Iris Marion Young

1949–2006

Désirée Lim

There are several important things to know about Iris Marion Young. The first is her remarkable career trajectory. Born in New York City in 1949, Young completed her master's degree and doctorate in philosophy at the Pennsylvania State University by the age of twenty-five. The following years of Young's life likewise proved to be extraordinarily productive. Before taking up her final position as professor in political science at the University of Chicago in 2000, she had established herself as one of the most important feminist thinkers in the world, a status merited by her influential insights on feminism, democracy and theories of justice.

At the same time, Young was a committed political activist. For her, theory and practice were inseparable. In her first, groundbreaking work, *Justice and the Politics of Difference* (1990), Young eschewed theories that were 'too abstract to be useful in evaluating actual institutions and practices.' She was admired throughout her career for her willingness to situate her ideas within concrete social realities. Theorists could not afford to stand away from the chaos and struggle of concrete political life. Tellingly, her book *Inclusion and Democracy* (2000) begins with the uncomfortable experience of soliciting signatures for a referendum petition in Pittsburgh on a freezing winter's day, a 'self-punishment' she persisted in because of her knowledge that many others were doing so. Driven by the importance of solidarity and collective action, Young participated in grassroots political activity for a striking multiplicity of social causes. These ranged from women's rights, the civil rights movement, various anti-war movements, debt relief for Africa, workers' rights, and the anti-nuclear power movement.

But there are other things you should know about Iris – things that take us a little closer to Iris Young the person, and not just the celebrated philosopher or passionate activist. She loved jazz music, frequenting bars around Chicago and playing jazz piano at the faculty club for her colleagues. When her daughter Morgan was born, Young brightly wrote to her friends, 'another socialist feminist has come into the world!' In this spirit, there is a story from Young's childhood that is worth recounting.

At the age of eleven, Young was unceremoniously taken to a teen-reform home with her brother and sister. Young's mother had been devastated by her husband's sudden death from a brain tumour. Shortly after, she was thrown in jail for child neglect – the primary evidence being 'drinking and a messy house'. While it was the first time Young's mother would be arrested, it was sadly not the last. She was soon marched away again after a small fire in their household revealed the 'papers strewn about and dust on the floor and beer cans'. Sent to live with a foster family, Young was only reunited with her mother after her foster father also died suddenly, instantly rendering her foster family a 'bad environment' for children in the eyes of the state.

Young candidly recalls this incident for a particular reason. In her essay 'House and Home: Feminist Variations on a Theme' (2005), she reflects upon the relationship between women and 'the home' under conditions of patriarchy. Here, Young agrees with other feminists like Luce Irigaray and Simone de Beauvoir that the 'home' can function as a source of oppression for women. After all, her mother was confined to the role of homemaker – a role that made her primarily responsible for mundane domestic chores. Rather than be free to carve out her own path, she was expected to carry out 'life maintenance' – 'cooking, cleaning, ironing and mending' for the sake of supporting her husband and children. Against this backdrop, Young's mother's imprisonment and separation from her children shows how cruel the penalties could be for women who dared to resist these expectations.

However, in calling attention to this part of Young's life, I have a different agenda. First of all, it disrupts the notion of the privileged childhood that philosophers are often presumed to share. This notion, I believe, is part and parcel of broader assumptions about *who philosophers are*: wealthy white men whose incipient genius is tenderly nurtured from a young age, and their scholarly pursuits blissfully uninterrupted by drudgery or poverty of any sort, much less being carted off to a teen-reform home.

More importantly, I wonder whether the difficulty of Young's early years did not so much serve as an obstacle to her intellectual flourishing as *shape* it. The above event starkly raises a number of deep philosophical questions, all of which Young was preoccupied with. This is a possibility that Karsten J. Struhl also raises in his touching 'Letter to Iris Young' (2009). As Struhl suggests, while we can never know the answer, we may still continue to construct an idea of who Iris Young was from her writings.

And even if Young's main theoretical concerns were inspired by an entirely different set of events, I believe that revisiting this childhood tragedy helps to anchor their importance. For these reasons, it is worth connecting a number of her central contributions to this part of her life story.

As a starting point, *Justice and the Politics of Difference* highlights the importance of social relations between persons for thinking about social justice. While taking care to acknowledge the significance of material inequality or deprivation, Young argues that there are other fundamental sources of injustice: namely *oppression* and *domination*. Oppression, for Young, is the 'institutional constraint on self-development'. People face oppression when they are subject to social conditions that prevent them from 'learning and using satisfying and expansive skills in socially recognised settings', or 'inhibit [their] ability to play and communicate with others or to express their feelings and perspective on social life in contexts where others can listen'. On the other hand, domination is the 'institutional constraint on self-determination'; we live within structures of domination if other people have the asymmetrical power to determine the conditions of our actions.

Why is it necessary to broaden our understanding of injustice? In having her children taken from her because of mere untidiness, Young's mother undeniably suffered immense injustice. And yet it did not stem from *material* deprivation. In 'House and Home' Young is careful to emphasise that they 'were not poor once the insurance and social security money came, just messy'. Rather, it seems that her mother was socially *oppressed* and *dominated* by those around her. In the first case, her ability to speak three languages and possession of a master's degree had already gone unrecognised; she had been judged solely in terms of how well she kept the house. On top of this, after her husband's death she was unable to communicate her grief to the neighbours, police and child-welfare agents, whether it was to ask for the emotional support she desperately needed, or to explain that her children remained well cared for despite the mess. In short, the social conditions of patriarchy blocked her from vital forms of self-development and self-expression. At the same time, unilateral decisions were made to place Young and her siblings in state and foster care. It seems that Young's mother was utterly unable to have a say in where *her* children should go. In this way, Young's social model of injustice helps us to understand what has gone wrong in such cases of parent–child separation.

Later, Young became interested in what she calls 'structural injustice'. In *Responsibility for Justice* (2011), her final book published after her death, she considers the fictional case of 'Sandy', a single mother who has been evicted from her apartment and is trying her best to find a new home to rent. The only affordable, decent and safe apartments Sandy locates are so far away from her workplace that she must devote some of her rent money to car payments. Furthermore, even though Sandy applies for a housing subsidy, she is told that the waiting time is about two years. In the end, Sandy has no choice but to take an apartment that is smaller than she hoped for. In the process, she faces one final obstacle: she must deposit three months' rent to secure the apartment, which is a typical landlord policy. Yet because she has used all her savings to pay for her car, she cannot rent the apartment, and now faces the looming prospect of homelessness.

This story, Young believes, 'can be repeated with minor variations for hundreds of thousands of people in the United States'. She contends that what happened to Sandy is not just unfortunate or inconvenient, but *morally wrong*. It is unjust for Sandy to be placed in her unenviable position. In order to make sense of this, Young thinks we need to fundamentally revise our presuppositions about what wrongdoing is. Typically, we regard ourselves as having suffered moral wrong when other individuals commit wrongs against us: for example, if Sandy became homeless because she was defrauded of her money by the landlord. You might also say that we are wronged when we are subject to a particular unjust law or policy, such as if Sandy was explicitly barred from renting apartments on the basis of her race. But, as Young notes, all the individuals that Sandy has interacted with (such as landlords and apartment-hunting agents) treat her decently, and she does not face the threat of homelessness because of a single unjust law. Rather, Sandy's position is the result of a particular *unjust social structure*, an outcome that is produced through the actions of masses of individuals acting in accordance with accepted norms and rules. Even if none of those individuals are guilty of committing wrongs against Sandy, nor do they actively intend to render Sandy homeless, the social structure they create through the sum of their actions nevertheless has a serious impact on her housing prospects. It sharply limits her choices, to the extent where she is basically unable to find a home for herself and her children. In other words, as Young powerfully argues, it is the social structure as a whole that we need to challenge, rather than seeking to blame any single person or policy.

While Young does not explicitly make the connection, the parallels with what happened to her mother are unmistakable. Like in Sandy's case, she suffered serious structural injustice – prolonged separation from her children – that happened as a result of individuals following the established rules and norms, such as the police and child protection services simply doing their jobs, and neighbours evaluating her behaviour in line with widely shared expectations of women. Young's discussion of these cases underscores not only the importance of working to change social structures, but also the necessity of critiquing our own daily actions and the social conditions they may inadvertently contribute to.

Young passed away suddenly from oesophageal cancer in 2006. Shortly before her death she was still travelling for lectures and conferences.

Young's body of work not only reveals how philosophy can serve to illuminate and give voice to lived experience – but also that it is made all the more nuanced and rich through its careful engagement with ordinary struggles. We would do well to follow her example.

Anita L. Allen

b. 1953

Ilhan Dahir

When asked where her hometown is, Anita Allen mentions Fort Worden, Washington, and Schofield Barracks in Hawaii before settling on Fort Benning, Georgia. 'It's where my parents are buried. I have an affection for the place,' she says in her 2017 interview with Clifford Sosis. It is important to note the many spaces a person can call home, the ability to see an essential familiarity in multiple places at once. It is the kind of awareness that permeates Anita Allen's sprawling scholarship. There is, at once, an ability to see broadly enough to make astute and novel observations about law and ethics in the contemporary age as well as such startling specificity as to contribute almost immediately to the canon of essential scholarship.

Anita Allen is widely known for her pioneering work in academia. Currently the Henry R. Silverman professor of law and professor of philosophy at the University of Pennsylvania Law School, she is perhaps best known as the creator of the privacy subfield within the discipline of philosophy. Her scholarship has yielded some of the essential texts on the topic. In fact, it is no exaggeration to say that there can be no complete discussion of contemporary philosophy about privacy without mention of her influence. Her books include *Uneasy Access: Privacy for Women in a Free Society* (1988), the first monograph on privacy written by an American philosopher, and the premier privacy law textbook *Privacy Law and Society* (2007), which has been called 'the most comprehensive textbook on the US law of privacy and data protection'. It is, to this day, unmatched in its breadth.

However, a chapter dedicated to Allen's scholarship is as much about her contribution to answering the unanswered questions as it is about how profoundly her work has impacted the questions we ask ourselves. Taking Gabriel García Márquez's conception that 'all human beings have three lives: public, private and secret', the question of privacy is made immediate and personal. The notion of a tripartite consciousness, operating between all human interactions but going largely unnamed, raises the stakes when it comes to examination of any one aspect of the lived experience. While the compartmentalisation of the self, keeping some facets of ourselves from the public or reserving some persona for the world, is a necessary part of daily life, new ethical enquiries present themselves within the digital age. How much of ourselves are we constructing across dimensions – public, private and secret – and how much ownership do we have over that self-construction? It seems, in a growingly connected world, anything and everything from social media, technological advances, smartphone applications and widespread internet usage is leading to the erosion of our ability to retain a genuine sense of privacy. Indeed, as Allen said in a speech at The Aspen Institute, 'The right to privacy has a foot in the grave.' However, this statement is not motivated by a pessimistic approach to the question of the future of privacy; rather, it is a clear-eyed assessment of the state of affairs as they stand. Allen's scholarship posits that the right to privacy, precarious as it may seem today, is a concept crucial to the experience of humanity. She boldly claims in *Unpopular Privacy: What Must We Hide?* (2011): 'Privacy is so important and so neglected in contemporary life that democratic states, though liberal and feminist, could be justified in undertaking a rescue mission that includes enacting paternalistic privacy laws for the benefit of uneager beneficiaries.' Allen does not simply examine the role of privacy in our lives but pushes against the parameters of the concept, asking which privacies people are dispositioned to protect, which they neglect, and what the role of good governance is in preserving this right.

As widely discussed as issues of privacy are today, the right to privacy is not a doctrinally protected concept. In fact, the 'right to privacy' as we have come to know it was first majorly discussed in the United States by Louis Brandeis and Samuel D. Warren in the 1890 *Harvard Law Review*, where they argued that, although it is not officially stated in the Bill of Rights – taking common law and the United States Constitution together – the case for a right to privacy could be made inferentially. Warren and Brandeis's article served as a turning point for the study of privacy, heralded by Harry Kalven Jr. (one of the most influential legal scholars of the twentieth century) as the 'most influential law review article of all'. It was one of the first attempts at summarising what the evasive term 'privacy' meant, while also endeavouring to define its often shifting borders. William Lloyd Prosser, a leading scholar on tort law, famously argued that such simplification would escape the point entirely, instead proposing that privacy was a collection of four separate torts (a wrongful act leading to legal liability): 1) appropriating the plaintiff's identity for the defendant's benefit, 2) placing the plaintiff in a false light in the public eye, 3) publicly disclosing private facts about the plaintiff, and 4) unreasonably intruding upon the seclusion or solitude of the plaintiff. All four of these general rules were unified only loosely by the concept known as the 'right to be left alone'.

However, it was Alan Westin's *Privacy and Freedom* (1967) and a 1980 *Yale Law Journal* article by Ruth Gavison that Allen credits with having inspired her work *Uneasy Access: Privacy for Women in a Free Society*. This would go on to be considered the first in-depth analysis of privacy by an academic philosopher and would set the stage for Allen's creation of the privacy subfield within philosophy. The book examines the meaning of privacy and the role it plays in modern life, while also containing a public policy approach missing from the work of her peers.

Allen's own education began at New College, a small liberal arts college in Sarasota where her interest in the humanities was fostered. It was at New College that she met her first mentors, the American pragmatist B. Gresham Riley, her continental philosophy professor Doug Berggren, and the analytic philosopher Bryan Norton who introduced her to Rudolf Carnap – the thinker who would inspire her undergraduate thesis on the rejection of metaphysics. It was with Norton's advice that she set her sights on a PhD. Shortly thereafter, Allen was admitted to the University of Michigan's philosophy department and she began her academic career. She received the Ford Fellowship to complete her doctoral work. After getting to Ann Arbor, her intellectual curiosity and academic achievement allowed her to quickly rise into positions of student leadership. Allen was elected graduate student representative to the faculty. She spent her time at the University of Michigan excelling academically while also making the most of every opportunity presented to her, even in the face of gendered and racialised discrimination – issues that would present themselves again when she set her sights on the workplace. In any case, she stated in her 2017 interview with Clifford Sosis that she 'made the best of things' and began her work as an educator at Carnegie Mellon University.

While discussions about privacy laws, privacy ethics and legal philosophy have grown tremendously in the modern era, Allen's specific approach has left an enduring mark. With the rapid growth in new technologies, the widening of the social sphere through the internet, and the expansion of the state's surveillance capacity, privacy discussions grow more and more complicated every year. Allen's book *Unpopular Privacy: What Must We Hide?* unpacks the moral considerations that communications technologies present in the way of privacy. Allen's seminal text *Uneasy Access* paved the way for discussions of privacy that delve into the multi-faceted nature of the concept, particularly focusing on the private–public distinction introduced by feminist thought leaders of the 1960s. The study of privacy, especially when understood in conjunction with law and ethics, has come a long way. An expert on privacy law, bioethics and the philosophy of privacy, Allen's scholarship on legal philosophy has played a role in propelling those fields forward.

In a world where developments in technology have greatly outpaced our progress in the protection of personal data, privacy has become a question inextricable from technology – how does a society maintain healthy rights preservation while encouraging technological improvement? Allen broaches this uncertain terrain in her 2013 article 'An Ethical Duty to Protect One's Own Information Privacy?' where she considers the matter from the angle of disclosure, pushing the discussion away from simply protecting information privacy to the more difficult moral question of whether individuals have a 'responsibility' or 'obligation' to protect their own privacy. In this way, privacy is a duty as much as a practice taken on by the citizen out of self-respect.

Through her work Allen has made it clear that the issue of privacy is one that holds ethical, political and social considerations within it all at once. It is for this reason that her work has resonated with those within the academy, while also establishing her as an expert and foremost thinker within other spheres. Her work was recognised by the highest office in the United States in 2010, when she was appointed by President Obama to the Presidential Commission for the Study of Bioethical Issues. This commission was set up by the Obama administration to serve in an advisory capacity on issues relating to bioethics.

A legal and philosophical scholar of exceptional skill, Allen's contributions to the field are doubled by the trailblazing effect her scholarship has already had on the academy. She is no stranger to firsts. The first African-American woman to hold both a PhD in philosophy and a law degree, the first Black woman to be the president of the Eastern Division of the American Philosophical Association, a National Academy of Medicine appointee, and one of the leading voices in privacy philosophy, she holds the double honour of opening the field for the women philosophers of tomorrow while profoundly contributing to the field today. In her Aspen Institute speech Allen continued that while 'the right to privacy has a foot in the grave . . . our grandchildren will resurrect privacy from a shallow grave'. When they dream of the 'solitude, independence of mind and confidentiality' that once existed with privacy, I believe they will call upon Allen's incisive scholarship to light the way. It is for this reason that I am optimistic for the future of privacy and for those who will resurrect it.

Azizah Y. al-Hibri
b. 1943

Nima Dahir

In the contemporary age, it is nearly impossible to read about Islamic jurisprudence, the theory or philosophy of law, without mention of the current contentious and divided global political climate. The discussion about the nature of this climate and what it can tell us about some of the major questions of the modern world is increasingly confused; it is a discourse that is necessarily multilayered. For this reason, the study of Islamic law requires political, ethical *and* philosophical analysis. While many thinkers have attempted to address the need for a multi-faceted and nuanced approach, this chapter is dedicated to the life and contributions of Azizah Y. al-Hibri – one of the great Islamic philosophers of the modern day. In a time of heightened discourse surrounding gender, Islam and their relationship, al-Hibri is a premier scholar at the juncture of women and Islam. Her work should be better recognised as a vital contribution to contemporary philosophy.

Azizah Y. al-Hibri is a Lebanese-American professor of law focused on human rights and Islamic jurisprudence. She graduated from the American University in Beirut with a bachelor's degree in philosophy in 1966. She then earned a PhD in philosophy at the University of Pennsylvania in 1975 and worked there as a philosophy professor, before later returning to study for a law degree in 1985. In 1992, upon being hired as an associate professor at the T. C. Williams School of Law at the University of Richmond, al-Hibri became the first Muslim woman to work as a law professor in the United States – an achievement that should not be understated.

Al-Hibri's research has focused on the intersection of Islamic law and gender equality. Much of her scholarship can be summarised in the pursuit of answering one question: how does Islamic jurisprudence fit into the twenty-first century? Throughout her career, her work has examined the creation and maintenance of Islamic law that is compatible with gender equality and human rights for all.

As such, al-Hibri has contributed significantly to the Islamic jurisprudence canon. Her work clarifies and defines the tenets of Islamic jurisprudence for legal audiences, while also critiquing the historical interpretations of religious text to further patriarchal status. Her work is crucial in the modern understanding of faith-based legal reasoning, as she examines the effects of patriarchy on how religion has been interpreted. In her 1997 article 'Islam, Law and Custom: Redefining Muslim Women's Rights', she asserts that much of Islamic jurisprudence that subjugates women (for example, rulings on divorce law, domestic violence and polygamy) is based on a patriarchal (and thus, faulty) interpretation. Al-Hibri's research instead maintains that the Islamic legal tradition is flexible enough to reflect the modern lives and beliefs of Muslim women.

A basic tenet of Islam is to accept the Quran as divinely ordained and as the unchanging word of God. Thus, the Quran serves as the primary religious text in the daily lives of Muslims and, importantly, for Islamic jurisprudence. Where the Quran is unclear, Muslim jurists turn to the sayings and actions of the prophet Muhammad (called *ahadith*). Both the Quran and the *ahadith* maintain the equality of all humans, and this has been interpreted to allow for the cultural customs of the society to weigh in. However, al-Hibri claims that too often cultural customs that are in conflict with the Quran and prophetic traditions are entrenched in the laws of Muslim countries. This confusion between culture and religious text threatens the autonomy of women in these countries and is difficult to extract because of a communal fear of questioning laws that seem to be based on religious interpretation. Al-Hibri claims that a lack of proper religious education perpetuates the confusion between culture and religion, and, in turn, the subjugation of women through these laws. Crucially, Islam has no formal clergy or hierarchical structure. Therefore, in the Islamic tradition, all Muslims with the required knowledge are allowed (and encouraged) to participate in their own reasoning and interpretation of religious text. Thus, many different and equally valid interpretations may exist.

Al-Hibri observes this phenomenon through a variety of different interpretations in the codified laws of nations in the Middle East. She examines the validity of these laws through the lens of Islamic jurisprudence and concludes that many are unduly influenced by patriarchy. Islamic interpretation is meant to adjust to the context of the particular society, which allows for flexible interpretation in a variety of different cultures, but also allows for patriarchal culture to interpret the work, helping to shape how it is understood and implemented.

The relationship that al-Hibri's work examines – between women and Islam – is one rooted in the past. Throughout Islamic history, various social and political conditions have deeply impacted how Islam is interpreted, and, in turn, how it is practised. Al-Hibri argues that while true Islam is not patriarchal, historical events have transformed the practice of Islam into patriarchy. The pre-Islamic period in the Arabian Peninsula (referred to as Jahiliyyah, or 'age of ignorance') was deeply steeped in patriarchal traditions, where female infanticide was fairly common, as was polygamy. Al-Hibri noted in her 1982 essay 'A Study of Islamic Herstory: Or how did we ever get into this mess?' how Islam fundamentally transformed the culture of the Arabian Peninsula by weakening the patriarchal hierarchy, replacing it with a religious relationship within which all are equal, regardless of gender, race, nationality or ethnicity. However, after the death of the Prophet, al-Hibri argues that culture re-entered religious discourse and, with it, patriarchy as well. Al-Hibri's job, then, is a crucial one: to re-examine what Islam might look like if liberated from the reins of patriarchy.

Al-Hibri has also written extensively on Muslim women's relationship to Western thought. More specifically, she has published numerous works on Western feminism and its relationship to the Muslim world, and, in turn, to Muslim women. She argues that colonisation changed much of the existing social structures in the Muslim world, exposing it to alternative religious beliefs and cultural values. However, al-Hibri does not concede to the superiority of Western values. Instead, she argues, Muslim women (and indeed, men) are faced with the problem of facilitating progress in their societies while maintaining their distinctive culture. She further argues that Western feminism, with its focus on secular assertions of women's rights, threatens losing sight of Muslim women both in the West and in Muslim-majority countries.

The relationship between Islamic and Western legal thought is also of interest to al-Hibri. Much of European legal thought, she argues, is inspired by Western contact with Islamic civilisation. She observes many similarities between the original founding premises of the United States and Islamic values, suggesting a borrowing of Islamic jurisprudence in the construction of the legal basis of the United States. From these observations, al-Hibri concludes democracy is quite compatible with Islamic values, and therefore the Muslim world can successfully engage with democratic experiments.

As a scholar of Islamic jurisprudence in the United States, al-Hibri occupies a unique academic space of increasing relevance. How do Muslim Americans fit into the greater American narrative? As a Lebanese immigrant to the US, al-Hibri speaks of her burgeoning desire to be an American as a young student. In her reading, the American values of separation of church and state, democracy, and constitutionally enshrined rights for all were reflected in the Islamic tradition, inspiring her career of research. Her work is shaped by a fundamental belief in the compatibility between American and Islamic values. As a result, in this time of heightened discourse around Muslims' place in the United States, al-Hibri's work is more important than ever. She carefully concludes that there is no fundamental dissonance between American and Muslim identities, and thus her work establishes in the canon what many American Muslims already know: they not only benefit from America, but the United States benefits from the propagation of Islamic values as well.

Having contributed significantly to academia, al-Hibri is also working to bridge the gap between her research and the real world. She founded KARAMAH: Muslim Women Lawyers for Human Rights, an organisation that promotes the scholarship and leadership of Muslim women, enabling them to facilitate positive change within their communities. She is also the founding editor of *Hypatia: A Journal of Feminist Philosophy*, which remains a very successful philosophy journal.

The work of Azizah Y. al-Hibri is dedicated to understanding the basis of Islamic legal jurisprudence and the ways it has been exacted in the subjugation of Muslim women. Her research and contributions have shaped much of the academic conversation around women in Islam and their relationship to their states, whether in the Muslim world or in the West. In an increasingly divided world that attempts to contrast Western and Islamic values, al-Hibri does the crucial scholarly work of bridging the gap between these value systems. As a trailblazer of Islamic jurisprudence and feminism, al-Hibri has contributed significantly to the philosophical canon on these relatively understudied topics. As a Muslim American woman myself, al-Hibri's innovative and necessary work on Islamic thought contributes to my own understandings of my faith and its practice in an American context. Religious scholarship flourishes under many interpretations, and as a trained philosopher, she provides an important exegesis of Islamic literature that builds upon and adds to my own Islamic readings. Her comparative work on Western and Islamic political, legal and historical thought has set the stage for further work. Al-Hibri's contributions to philosophy and law are innumerable and significant.

Further Resources

DIOTIMA

Recommended Further Reading

Allen, R. E., *Plato's Symposium*, New Haven: Yale University Press, 1991

Keime, Christian, 'The Role of Diotima in the Symposium: The Dialogue and Its Double', in Gabriele Cornelli (ed.), *Plato's Styles and Characters: Between Literature and Philosophy*, Berlin: De Gruyter, 2015, 379–400

Nails, Debra, *The People of Plato: A Prosopography of Plato and Other Socratics*, Indianapolis: Hackett Publishing, 2002

Neumann, Harry, 'Diotima's Concept of Love', *American Journal of Philology*, Vol. 86(1), 1965, 33–59

Nye, Andrea, 'The Subject of Love: Diotima and Her Critics', *Journal of Value Inquiry*, Vol. 24, 1990, 135–153

Nye, Andrea, 'The Hidden Host: Irigaray and Diotima at Plato's Symposium', *Hypatia*, Vol. 3(3), 1989, 45–61

Nye, Andrea, *Socrates and Diotima: Sexuality, Religion, and the Nature of Divinity*, Palgrave Macmillan, 2015

BAN ZHAO

Primary Texts

Swann, Nancy Lee, *Pan Chao: Foremost Woman Scholar of China*, Ann Arbor: Center for Chinese Studies, University of Michigan, 1932 (republished 2001)

Tiwald, Justin and Van Norden, Bryan W. (eds.), *Readings in Later Chinese Philosophy: Han to the 20th Century*, Indianapolis: Hackett, 2014

Wang, Yanti (ed.) *Zhongguo Gudai Nvzuojia Ji*, Jinan: Shandong University Press, 1999

Recommended Further Reading

Chen, Yu-Shih, 'The Historical Template of Pan Chao's *Nü Chieh*,' *T'oung Pao*, Second Series, Vol. 82, 1996, 229–257

Goldin, Paul R., *After Confucius: Studies in Early Chinese Philosophy*, Honolulu: University of Hawaii Press, 2005

Lee, Lily Xiao Hong, *The Virtue of Yin: Studies on Chinese Women*, Sydney: Wild Peony, 1994

Van Gulik, Robert Hans, *Sexual Life in Ancient China: A Preliminary Survey of Chinese Sex and Society from ca. 1500 BC till 1644 AD*, Leiden and Boston: Brill, 2002

HYPATIA

Primary Texts

Scholasticus, Socrates, *The Ecclesiastical History*, c. 440

The letters of Synesius, Bishop of Ptolemais, c. 394–413

Damascius, *Life of Isidore*, c. 530

Recommended Further Reading

Deakin, Michael A.B., *Hypatia of Alexandria: Mathematician and Martyr*, Amherst: Promethius Books, 2007

Dzielska, Maria, *Hypatia of Alexandria (Revealing Antiquity)*, Cambridge: Harvard University Press, 1996

History Chicks Podcast, 'Episode 95: Hypatia of Alexandria'

Russell, Dora, *Hypatia: or, Woman and Knowledge*, Folcroft Library Editions, 1976

Watts, Edward J., *Hypatia: The Life and Legend of an Ancient Philosopher*, Oxford: Oxford University Press, 2017

LALLA

Primary Texts

Hoskote, Ranjit, (trans.), *I, Lalla: The Poems of Lal Ded*, New Delhi:
Penguin Books, 2011

Recommended Further Reading

Kachru, Sonam, 'The Words of Lalla: Voices of the Everyday Wild',
Spolia Magazine, The Medieval Issue, No. 5, 2013

Kak, Jaishree, *Mystical Verse of Lallā: A Journey of Self-Realization*,
Delhi: Motilal Banarsidass, 2007

Toshkhani, Shashishekhar (ed.), *Lal Ded: The Great Kashmiri
Saint-Poetess*, New Delhi: A.P.H. Publishing Corporation, 2000

Voss Roberts, Michelle, 'Power, Gender, and the Classification of a
Kashmir Śaiva "Mystic"', *Journal of Hindu Studies*, Vol. 3, 2010,
279–297

MARY ASTELL

Primary Texts

Astell, Mary, *Political Writings*, Patricia Springborg (ed.), Cambridge:
Cambridge University Press, 1996

— *A Serious Proposal to the Ladies*, Patricia Springborg (ed.),
Peterborough: Broadview Press, 2002

— *The Christian Religion, as Professed by a Daughter of the Church
of England*, Jacqueline Broad (ed.), 'The Other Voice in Early
Modern Europe – The Toronto Series', Vol. 24, 2013

— Astell, Mary, and Norris, John, *Letters Concerning the Love of God*,
E. Derek Taylor and Melvyn New (eds.), London: Routledge,
2005

Recommended Further Reading

Broad, Jacqueline, *Women Philosophers of the Seventeenth Century*,
Cambridge: Cambridge University Press, 2003

— *The Philosophy of Mary Astell: An Early Modern Theory of Virtue*,
Oxford: Oxford University Press, 2015

Perry, Ruth, *The Celebrated Mary Astell: An Early English Feminist*, Chicago: University of Chicago Press, 1986

— 'Astell, Mary (1666–1731), philosopher and promoter of women's education', *Oxford Dictionary of National Biography*, Oxford: Oxford University Press, 2009

Sowaal, Alice and Weiss, Penny, (eds.) *Feminist Interpretations of Mary Astell*, University Park, Pennsylvania: Pennsylvania State University Press, 2016

Webb, Simone, 'Mary Astell's *A Serious Proposal to the Ladies*', *1000-Word Philosophy: An Introductory Anthology*, 2018

MARY WOLLSTONECRAFT

Primary Texts

Wollstonecraft, Mary, *Thoughts on the Education of Daughters: With Reflections on Female Conduct, in the More Important Duties of Life*, London: Joseph Johnson, 1787

— *Mary: A Fiction*, 1788, New York: Garland Press, 1974

— *Original Stories from Real Life: with Conversations Calculated to Regulate the Affections and Form the Mind to Truth and Goodness*, London: Joseph Johnson, 1788

— *A Vindication of the Rights of Men*, 1790, in Janet Todd (ed.), *Political Writings: A Vindication of the Rights of Men, A Vindication of the Rights of Woman and an Historical and Moral View of the French Revolution*, (republished by Oxford University Press, 2008)

— *A Vindication of the Rights of Woman*, 1792, in Todd, 2008 (see above)

— *An Historical and Moral View of the Origin and Progress of the French Revolution and the Effect it Has Produced in Europe*, 1794, in Todd, 2008 (see above)

— *Letters Written During a Short Residence in Sweden, Norway and Denmark*, 1795, in Ingrid Horrocks (ed.), Broadview Press, 2013

— *Maria: or, the Wrongs of Woman*, fragment, begun in 1796. In Godwin, 1798 (see below)

— *The Memoirs and Posthumous Works of the Author of A Vindication of the Rights of Woman*, William Godwin (ed.), London: Joseph Johnson, 1798; Gina Luria (ed.), New York: Garland Press, 1974

Recommended Further Reading

Bergès, Sandrine, *The Routledge Guidebook to Wollstonecraft's A Vindication of the Rights of Woman*, London and New York: Routledge, 2013

Halldenius, Lena, *Mary Wollstonecraft and Feminist Republicanism: Independence, Rights and the Experience of Unfreedom*, London: Pickering & Chatto, 2015

Todd, Janet, *Mary Wollstonecraft: A Revolutionary Life*, London: Weidenfeld & Nicolson, 2000

HARRIET TAYLOR MILL

Primary Texts

Taylor Mill, Harriet, *The Complete Works of Harriet Taylor Mill*, Jo Ellen Jacobs (ed.), Indiana: Indiana University Press, 1998

Stuart Mill, John, *On Liberty*, *Collected Works* XVIII, Toronto: University of Toronto Press, 1977

Stuart Mill, John, *On Marriage*, *CW* XXI, Toronto: University of Toronto Press, 1984

Stuart Mill, John, *Principles of Political Economy*, *CW* II and III, Toronto: University of Toronto Press, 1965

Stuart Mill, John, *Autobiography*, *CW* I, Toronto: University of Toronto Press, 1981

Recommended Further Reading

Jacobs, Jo Ellen, ' "The Lot of Gifted Ladies is Hard" A Study of Harriet Taylor Mill Criticism', *Hypatia*, Vol. 9(3), 1994

McCabe, Helen H, 'Harriet Taylor Mill', *A Companion to Mill*, London: Blackwell, 2016

Miller, David, 'Harriet Taylor Mill', *Stanford Encyclopaedia of Philosophy*

GEORGE ELIOT (MARY ANNE EVANS)

Primary Texts

Eliot, George, *Middlemarch*, 1871; Penguin, 1994
— *Silas Marner*, 1861; Penguin, 2003

Recommended Further Reading

Ashton, Rosemary, *George Eliot: A Life*, Penguin, 1998
Carlisle, Clare, 'Introduction' to *Spinoza's Ethics, Translated by George Eliot*, Princeton: Princeton University Press, 2019
Uglow, Jenny, *George Eliot*, Virago, 1987

EDITH STEIN

Primary Texts

Stein, Edith, *On the Problem of Empathy*, Waltraut Stein (trans.), Washington, D.C.: ICS Publications, 1989
— *Finite and Eternal Being*, Kurt F. Reinhardt (trans.), Washington, D.C.: ICS Publications, 2006

Recommended Further Reading

Husserl, Edmund, *On the Phenomenology of the Consciousness of Internal Time*, John Barnett Brough (trans.); Dordrecht, Boston and London: Kluwer, 1991 [see Brough's introduction in particular for a more in-depth history of the development of the text and Stein's contribution]
McDaniel, Kris, 'Edith Stein: On the Problem of Empathy', in *Ten Neglected Classics of Philosophy*, Eric Schliesser (ed.), Oxford: Oxford University Press, 2016
Ricci, Gabriel R., 'Husserl's Assistants: Phenomenology Reconstituted', *History of European Ideas*, Vol. 36, 2010, 419–426

HANNAH ARENDT

Primary Texts

Arendt, Hannah, *The Origins of Totalitarianism*, New York: Harcourt Brace Jovanovich, 1951
— *The Human Condition*, Chicago: University of Chicago Press, 1958
— *Eichmann in Jerusalem: A Report on the Banality of Evil*, New York: Viking Press, 1963 (revised and enlarged edition, 1965)
— *On Revolution*, New York: Viking Press, 1965
— *Men in Dark Times*, New York: Harcourt Brace Jovanovich, 1968
— *On Violence*, New York: Harcourt Brace Jovanovich, 1970

Recommended Further Reading

Benhabib, Seyla, *The Reluctant Modernism of Hannah Arendt*, Thousand Oaks: Sage, 1996
Bernstein, Richard J., *Why Read Hannah Arendt Now*, London: Polity Press, 2018
Habermas, Jürgen, 'Hannah Arendt: On the Concept of Power', in *Philosophical-Political Profiles*, London: Heinemann, 1983
Heller, Anne C., *Hannah Arendt: A Life in Dark Times*, Amazon Publishing, 2015

SIMONE DE BEAUVOIR

Primary Texts

De Beauvoir, Simone, *She Came to Stay*, 1943, Yvonne Moyse and Roger Senhouse (trans.), London: Harper Perennial, 2006
— *Pyrrhus and Cinéas*, 1944, Marybeth Timmerman (trans.), in *Philosophical Writings*, Margaret Simons with Marybeth Timmerman and Mary Beth Mader (eds.), Chicago: University of Illinois Press, 2004
— *The Ethics of Ambiguity*, 1948, Bernard Frechtman (trans.), New York: Citadel Press, 1976

— *The Second Sex*, 1949, Constance Borde and Sheila Malovany-Chevallier (trans.), London: Vintage, 2009

— *The Mandarins*, 1954, Leonard M. Friedman (trans.), London: Harper Perennial, 2005

— *Memoirs of a Dutiful Daughter*, 1958, James Kirkup (trans.), London: Penguin, 2001

Recommended Further Reading

Kirkpatrick, Kate, *Becoming Beauvoir: A Life*, London: Bloomsbury, 2019

Simons, Margaret, *The Philosophy of Simone de Beauvoir: Critical Essays*, Bloomington: Indiana University Press, 2006

Stanford, Stella, *How to Read Beauvoir*, London: Granta, 2006

IRIS MURDOCH

Primary Texts

Murdoch, Iris, *Sartre: Romantic Rationalist*, Cambridge: Bowes and Bowes, 1953

Murdoch, Iris & Hepbern R. W, 'Symposium: Vision and Choice in Morality', Proceedings of the Aristotelian Society, Supplementary Volumes, Vol. 30, Dreams and Self-Knowledge, 1956, 14–58

Murdoch, Iris, 'The Sublime and the Good', *Chicago Review*, 1959

— *The Sovereignty of Good*, London: Routledge & Kegan Paul, 1970

— *Metaphysics as a Guide to Morals*, London: Penguin, 1992

Recommended Further Reading

Bayley, John, *Elegy for Iris*, New York: Picador, 1999

Broackes, Justin (ed.), *Iris Murdoch, Philosopher*, Oxford: Oxford University Press, 2012

Conradi, Peter J., *Iris Murdoch: A Life*, London: W.W. Norton & Co., 2001

Mac Cumhaill, Clare, and Wiseman, Rachael, In Parenthesis project, Durham University (http://www.womeninparenthesis.co.uk)

Nussbaum, Martha, 'When She Was Good', *The New Republic*, 2001

MARY MIDGLEY

Primary Texts

Midgley, Mary, *Beast and Man: The Roots of Human Nature*, London: Routledge Classics, 1979

— *Heart and Mind: The Varieties of Moral Experience*, London: Routledge Classics, 1981

— *Animals and Why They Matter*, Athens: University of Georgia Press, 1983

— *Evolution as a Religion: Strange Hopes and Stranger Fears*, London: Methuen & Co., 1985

— *Science as Salvation: A Modern Myth and its Meaning*, London: Routledge Classics, 1994

— *Utopias, Dolphins and Computers: Problems of Philosophical Plumbing*, London: Routledge Classics, 1996

— *Science and Poetry*, London: Routledge Classics, 2001

— *The Owl of Minerva: A Memoir*, London: Routledge Classics, 2005

— *The Solitary Self: Darwin and the Selfish Gene*, London: Routledge Classics, 2010

— *The Myths We Live By*, London: Routledge Classics, 2011

— *What Is Philosophy For?*, London: Bloomsbury Academic, 2018

Recommended Further Reading

Foot, Philippa, *Natural Goodness*, Oxford: Clarendon Press, 2001

Kidd, Ian James and McKinnell, Liz (eds.), *Science and the Self: Animals, Evolution and Ethics: Essays in Honour of Mary Midgley*, London: Routledge, 2016

Mac Cumhaill, Clare and Wiseman, Rachael, 'A Female School of Analytic Philosophy? Anscombe, Foot, Midgley and Murdoch', 2018, available at www.womeninparenthesis.co.uk

Midgley, David, *The Essential Mary Midgley*, London: Routledge, 2005

Warnock, Mary, *Women Philosophers*, London: J.M. Dent & Sons Ltd, 1996

For more information on Midgley and her contemporaries visit the In Parenthesis project website: www.womeninparenthesis.co.uk

ELIZABETH ANSCOMBE

Primary Texts

Wittgenstein, Ludwig, *Philosophical Investigations*, Elizabeth Anscombe (trans.), Oxford: Basil Blackwell, 1953

Anscombe, Elizabeth, *Intention*, Oxford: Basil Blackwell, 1957; second edition, 1963.

— 'Modern Moral Philosophy', *Philosophy*, Vol. 33(124), 1958, 1–19

— *An Introduction to Wittgenstein's Tractatus*, London: Hutchinson University Library, 1959

— *Three Philosophers: Aristotle, Aquinas, Frege*, with Peter Geach, Oxford: Basil Blackwell, 1961

Recommended Further Reading

Driver, Julia, 'Gertrude Elizabeth Margaret Anscombe', *The Stanford Encyclopedia of Philosophy* (Spring 2018 edition), Edward N. Zalta (ed.)

Ford, Anton, Jennifer Hornsby, and Frederick Stoutland (eds.), *Essays on Anscombe's Intention*, Cambridge, MA: Harvard University Press, 2011

Teichman, J., 'Gertrude Elizabeth Margaret Anscombe 1919–2001', in *Proceedings of the British Academy*, Vol. 115, *Biographical Memoirs of Fellows, I*, British Academy.

Teichmann, R. (ed.), *The Philosophy of Elizabeth Anscombe*, Oxford: Oxford University Press, 2008

MARY WARNOCK

Primary Texts

Warnock, Mary, *An Intelligent Person's Guide to Ethics*, London: Gerald Duckworth & Co. Ltd., 1998

— *A Memoir: People and Places*, London: Gerald Duckworth & Co. Ltd., 2002

— *Making Babies: Is There a Right to Have Children?*, Oxford: Oxford University Press, 2003

— *Ethics Since 1900*, Edinburgh: Axios Press, 2007

Recommended Further Reading

Panitch, Vida, 'Global Surrogacy: Exploitation to Empowerment',
Journal of Global Ethics, Vol. 9(3), 2013, 329–43

Wilkinson, Stephen, 'The Exploitation Argument against
Commercial Surrogacy', *Bioethics*, Vol. 17(2), 2003, 169–187

Wilkinson, Stephen, 'Exploitation in International Paid Surrogacy
Arrangements', *Journal of Applied Philosophy*, Vol. 33(2), 2016,
125–45

Wilson, Duncan, 'Creating the "ethics industry": Mary Warnock,
in vitro fertilization and the history of bioethics in Britain',
Biosocieties, Vol. 6(20), 2011, 121–141

Surrogacy Arrangements Act 1985

SOPHIE BOSEDE OLUWOLE

Primary Texts

Oluwole, Sophie, *Readings in African Philosophy*, Lagos: Masstech
Publishers, 1989

— *Witchcraft, Reincarnation and the God Head (Issues in African
Philosophy)*, Excel, 1992

— *Womanhood in Yoruba Traditional Thought*, Iwalewa-Haus, 1993

— *Philosophy and Oral Tradition*, Lagos: African Research
Konsultancy, 1995

— *Democratic Patterns and Paradigms: Nigerian Women's Experience*,
Lagos: Goethe Institute, 1996

— 'African Philosophy on the Threshold of Modernisation':
Valedictory Lecture, First Academic Publishers, 2007

— *African Myths and Legends of Gender* (co-authored with J. O. Akin
Sofoluwe), Lagos: African Research Konsultancy, 2014

— *Socrates and Orunmila: Two Patrons of Classical Philosophy*, Lagos:
African Research Konsultancy, 2015

Recommended Further Reading

Fayemi, Ademola Kazeem, 'Sophie Oluwole's Hermeneutic Trend
in African Political Philosophy: Some Comments', *Hermeneia*,
2013

Kelani, Tunde, 'Oro Isiti with Professor Sophie Oluwole' (documentary series), 2016

Kimmerle, Heinz, 'An Amazing Piece of Comparative Philosophy', in *Filosofia Theoretica: Journal of African Philosophy, Culture and Religions*, Vol. 3(2), 2014

Oluwole, Sophie, 'The Cultural Enslavement of the African Mind', in Jeje Kolawole (ed.), *Introduction to Social and Political Philosophy*, 2001

ANGELA DAVIS

Primary Texts

Angela Y. Davis, (ed.), *If They Come in the Morning: Voices of Resistance*, New Jersey: Third World Press, 1971

— *Angela Davis: An Autobiography*, New York: Random House, 1974

— *Women, Race & Class*, New York: Random House, 1981

— *Women, Culture & Politics*, New York: Random House, 1990

— *The Angela Y. Davis Reader*, Joy James (ed.), Malden, MA: Blackwell, 1998

— *Are Prisons Obsolete?*, New York: Seven Stories Press, 2003

— Interview in *The Black Power Mixtape 1967–1975*, Göran Olsson (dir.), IFC Films, 2011

— *The Meaning of Freedom, And Other Difficult Dialogues*, San Francisco: City Lights Books, 2012

— *Freedom is a Constant Struggle: Ferguson, Palestine and the Foundations of a Movement*, Frank Barat (ed.), Chicago: Haymarket Books, 2016

— 'Statement on the Birmingham Civil Rights Institute', January 7 2019

IRIS MARION YOUNG

Primary Texts

Marion Young, Iris, *Justice and the Politics of Difference*, Princeton, New Jersey: Princeton University Press, 1990

— *Intersecting Voices: Dilemmas of Gender, Political Philosophy and Policy*, Princeton, New Jersey: Princeton University Press, 1997

— *Inclusion and Democracy*, Oxford, New York: Oxford University Press, 2000

— *Global Challenges: War, Self-Determination and Responsibility for Justice*, Cambridge; Malden, Massachusetts: Polity, 2007

— *Responsibility for Justice*, Oxford: Oxford University Press, 2011

Marion Young, Iris, and Jaggar, Alison M. (eds.), *A Companion to Feminist Philosophy*, Malden, Massachusetts: Blackwell, 2000

Recommended Further Reading

Alcoff, Linda M., 'Dreaming of Iris', *Philosophy Today*, Vol. 52, 2008

Ferguson, Ann, and Nagel, Mechtild (eds.), *Dancing with Iris: The Philosophy of Iris Marion Young*, Oxford: Oxford University Press, 2009

La Caze, Marguerite, 'Iris Marion Young's Legacy for Feminist Theory', *Philosophy Compass*, Vol. 9(7), 2014

ANITA L. ALLEN

Primary Texts

Allen, Anita L., *Uneasy Access: Privacy for Women in a Free Society*, Lanham, Maryland: Rowman & Littlefield, 1988

— *Why Privacy Isn't Everything: Feminist Reflections on Personal Accountability*, Lanham, Maryland: Rowman & Littlefield, 2003

— *The New Ethics: A Guided Tour of the Twenty-First Century Moral Landscape*, New York: Miramax Books, 2004

— 'Forgetting yourself', in Cudd, Ann E., Andreasen, Robin O., *Feminist Theory: A Philosophical Anthology*, Oxford, UK; Malden, Massachusetts: Blackwell Publishing, 2005, 352–364

— *Unpopular Privacy: What Must We Hide? (Studies in Feminist Philosophy)*, Oxford: Oxford University Press, 2011

Allen, Anita L. and Regan, Jr., Milton C., (eds.), *Debating 'Democracy's Discontent': Essays on American Politics, Law, and Public Philosophy*, Oxford: Oxford University Press, 1998

Allen, Anita L. and Turkington, Richard C., *Privacy Law: Cases and Materials*, Eagan, Minnesota: West Group, 2002

Recommended Further Reading

Sosis, Clifford, 'What Is It Like to Be a Philosopher?', September 2017, www.whatisitliketobeaphilosopher.com/anita-allen
Yancy, George, 'The Pain and Promise of Black Women in Philosophy', June 2018 https://www.nytimes.com/2018/06/18/opinion/black-women-in-philosophy.html
Yancy, George, *African-American Philosophers: 17 Conversations*, New York: Routledge, 1998

AZIZAH Y. AL-HIBRI

Primary Texts

Al-Hibri, Azizah Y., *Women and Islam*, Oxford: Pergamon Press, 1982
— 'A Study of Islamic Herstory: Or How Did We Ever Get Into This Mess?' In *Women's Studies International Forum*, Vol. 5(2), 1982, 207–219
— *Islamic Constitutionalism and the Concept of Democracy*, 24 Case W. Res. j. Int'l L., 1, 1992
— 'Islam, Law and Custom: Redefining Muslim Women's Rights', *American University International Law Review*, Vol. 12(1), 1997, 1–44
— 'Islamic and American Constitutional Law: Borrowing Possibilities or a History of Borrowing?', *U. Pa. J. Const. L.*, *1*, 492, 1998
— 'Is Western Patriarchal Feminism Good for Third World/Minority Women?', in *Is Multiculturalism Bad for Women?* by Susan Moller Okin, Princeton: Princeton University Press, 1999
— 'An Introduction to Muslim Women's Rights', in *Windows of Faith: Muslim Women Scholar-Activists in North America*, Gisela Webb (ed.), Syracuse: Syracuse University Press, 2000
— 'Muslim Women's Rights in the Global Village: Challenges and Opportunities', *Journal of Law and Religion*, Vol. 15, 2001, 37–66

Recommended Further Reading

Al-Hibri, Azizah Y., Carter, S., Gabel, P. and O'Hare, J., Panel
Discussion: Does Religious Faith Interfere with a Lawyer's Work?
Fordham Urban Law Journal, Vol. 26, 1999, 985–1018

Interview with Azizah Y. al-Hibri, on *NOW with Bill Moyers*, New
York: WNET, 2002

Haddad, Yvonne Y., 'The Post-9/11 "Hijab" as Icon', *Sociology of
Religion*, Vol. 68(3), 2007, 253–267

More Philosopher Queens

There have been hundreds, if not thousands, of women philosophers throughout history but we could only fit twenty into this book. So here is a list of a few more Philosopher Queens for you to research and enjoy.

Gargi Vachaknavi
Themistoclea
Theano of Croton
Hipparchia of Maroneia
Nicarete of Megara
Ptolemais of Cyrene
Aesara of Lucania
Xie Daoyun
Saint Catherine of Alexandria
Sosipatra of Ephesus
Aedesia
Héloïse d'Argenteuil
Hildegard of Bingen
Akka Mahadevi
Saint Catherine of Siena
Tullia d'Aragona
Teresa of Ávila
Moderata Fonte

Bathsua Makin
Anna Maria van Schurman
Catharine Trotter Cockburn
Elisabeth of Bohemia
Margaret Cavendish
Anne Conway
Gabrielle Suchon
Sor Juana Inés de la Cruz
Damaris Masham
Lady Ranelagh (Katherine Jones)
Émilie du Châtelet
Olympe de Gouges
Sophie de Condorcet
Lady Mary Shepherd
Nana Asma'u
Flora Tristán of Perú
Victoria Welby

Ida B. Wells
Olga Hahn-Neurath
Susan Stebbing
Hélène Metzger
Susanne Langer
Sofya Yanovskaya
Maria Kokoszyńska-
    Lutmanowa
Margaret MacDonald
Simone Weil
Margaret Masterman
Elizabeth Lane Beardsley
Philippa Foot
Ruth Barcan Marcus
Verena Huber-Dyson
Sylvia Wynter
Judith Jarvis Thomson
Virginia Held
Amélie Rorty
Susan Sontag
Audre Lorde
Margaret P. Battin
Anita Silvers
Hidé Ishiguro
Dorothy Edgington
Uma Chakravarti
Onora O'Neill
Sarah Broadie
Gayatri Chakravorty Spivak
Patricia Churchland

Rosalind Hursthouse
Nancy Cartwright
Susan Haack
Susan Moller Okin
Eva Kittay
Linda Zagzebski
Martha Nussbaum
Adriana Cavarero
Patricia Hill Collins
Margaret Urban Walker
Gail Fine
Sally Haslanger
Seyla Benhabib
Christine Korsgaard
bell hooks
Susan Wolf
Jean Hampton
Rosi Braidotti
Judith Butler
Elizabeth Anderson
Christina Sharpe
Rae Langton
Angie Hobbs
Miranda Fricker
Jasbir Puar
Jennifer Saul
Sara Ahmed
Cécile Fabre
Kathryn Sophia Belle
Kate Manne

Acknowledgements

When we first had the idea for *The Philosopher Queens* following a disheartening trip to the local bookshop, nothing could have prepared us for the journey of the last two years. We cannot do justice in this short space to all the people who have helped us; however, there are a few who deserve particular mention.

We would like to begin by thanking all those who supported our crowdfunding campaign for this book. *The Philosopher Queens* only exists due to the faith and encouragement of all the pledgers, and we feel very lucky to have shared this journey with you.

This project would have been impossible without the incredible support and friendship from our dream team of women at Unbound: Katy Guest, DeAndra Lupu and Georgia Odd, and our ludicrously talented illustrator Emmy Smith. Thank you for taking a chance on us and for your enthusiasm for this book, which kept us all working hard right to the very end.

There are also many people who offered support by commenting on drafts and providing academic expertise to help make the book rigorous as well as accessible: Kim Henningsen, Samantha Rose Hill, Mary Townsend, Theo Kwek, Mia Tong and Jade (Ngoc) Huynh. We would also like to thank Vivek Kembaiyan who assisted Professor Allen in drafting her chapter on Angela Davis.

As always, projects like this are shared ventures with family and friends. To our wonderful parents, housemates, colleagues and friends, and everyone who listened to our fears, frustrations and excitement: thank you. A particular shout-out to the fearless women in our lives who provide a constant source of inspiration. Rebecca would also like to thank her better half Ivan, who is a constant source of support, encouragement and joy. Lisa would particularly like to thank her mum Charyl and sister Ali for being her first and most precious feminist role models.

The final thank you goes to our first philosophy teachers, Matthew Kelly and Gabrielle Crisp. Without them, and friendships that grew from our classes with them, including our own, we would not have studied philosophy and become the women we are today. Thank you.

About the Authors

ZOI ALIOZI is a human rights scholar-activist. She is an academic, an awarded philosopher and an international human rights lawyer. Her research interests include human rights, law, philosophy, activism, feminism, climate change, aesthetics, arts and cinematography.

ANITA L. ALLEN is the Henry R. Silverman professor of law and professor of philosophy at the University of Pennsylvania Law School. She is an expert on privacy law, the philosophy of privacy, bioethics and contemporary values, and is recognised for scholarship about legal philosophy, women's rights and race relations.

GULZAAR BARN is a postdoctoral research associate at King's College London. Prior to this, she was a lecturer in philosophy at the University of Birmingham. She holds a DPhil in philosophy from the University of Oxford. Her doctoral studies were funded by the Wellcome Trust, and during this time she also undertook a postgraduate research fellowship at the Parliamentary Office of Science and Technology in Westminster, London.

SANDRINE BERGÈS is an associate professor at Bilkent University. She is an active member of Project Vox and the

New Narratives Project international groups striving to reintroduce important texts by women philosophers into teaching and research. She is also the co-founder of the Turkish-European Network for the Study of Women Philosophers and of SWIP-TR.

REBECCA BUXTON is a DPhil student at the University of Oxford, working on political philosophy and forced migration. Her research in particular looks at the political rights of refugees and migrants. Rebecca completed her BA in philosophy at King's College London and her MSc in Refugee and Forced Migration Studies at the University of Oxford.

CLARE CARLISLE is professor of philosophy and theology at King's College London. She studied at Trinity College, Cambridge, obtaining her BA in Philosophy in 1998 and her PhD in 2002. Since then she has published four books on Kierkegaard, one book on habit, the first English edition of Félix Ravaisson's *De l'habitude*, and George Eliot's translation of Spinoza's *Ethics*.

HANNAH CARNEGY-ARBUTHNOTT works on topics in political philosophy, moral philosophy and feminist philosophy. She completed her MPhil and PhD in philosophy at University College London, and held postdoctoral positions at Stanford's McCoy Family Center for Ethics in Society and at the Centre de recherche en éthique in Montreal.

ILHAN DAHIR is a writer and researcher currently working on her second master's degree in Global Governance and Diplomacy at the University of Oxford. She was awarded a Rhodes Scholarship in 2016 and completed a master's degree in Refugee and Forced Migration Studies in 2017.

NIMA DAHIR is a PhD student in sociology at Stanford University studying inequality in immigrant communities. She graduated summa cum laude from the Ohio State University with degrees in mathematics and economics. She has previously worked as an analyst at the Federal Reserve Bank of New York. Nima is a co-founder of Refuge, an organisation centred on mentoring young adult refugees.

JAE HETTERLEY is a graduate student in philosophy at the University of Warwick. The primary focus of her research concerns the history of metaphysics and phenomenology, and in particular the work of Immanuel Kant and Martin Heidegger. She is also interested in analysing how phenomenology can be used as a methodology for understanding the lived experiences of minority groups.

KATE KIRKPATRICK is Fellow in Philosophy and Christian Ethics at Regent's Park College, University of Oxford. She was previously a lecturer in Religion, Philosophy and Culture at King's College London. She has taught 'The Philosophy and Feminism of Simone de Beauvoir' for the University of Oxford's master's degree in Women's Studies, and is the author of several books and articles on Beauvoir, Sartre and existentialism.

DÉSIRÉE LIM is an assistant professor of philosophy at the Department of Philosophy in Penn State. She is also a research associate at the Rock Ethics Institute. Désirée was previously a postdoctoral fellow at Stanford University's McCoy Center for Ethics in Society. She completed her PhD in philosophy at King's College London in June 2016.

EVA KIT WAH MAN is a professor of Religion and Philosophy at Hong Kong Baptist University. She completed her PhD in Chinese Studies (Aesthetics) at the Chinese University of Hong Kong, and her MPhil in philosophy at the same institution.

HELEN MCCABE is an assistant professor in political theory at the University of Nottingham. Helen's research has mainly looked at the political philosophy of John Stuart Mill, especially his connections to pre-Marxist socialism. In 2018 Helen became director of Disposable Brides, which is part of the Rights Lab initiative, a University of Nottingham Beacon of Excellence project on forced marriage.

FAY NIKER is an assistant professor of philosophy at the University of Stirling in Scotland, where she works on topics in social and political philosophy and in applied ethics. She was previously a postdoctoral fellow at Stanford University's McCoy Center for Ethics in Society, and before that Fay completed her PhD in political theory at the University of Warwick.

ELLIE ROBSON is a philosophy master's student at Durham University, where she also completed her undergraduate degree. Focusing primarily on the philosophy of Mary Midgley, Ellie works mainly on twentieth-century women in philosophy, exploring themes of ethical naturalism and human nature.

MINNA SALAMI is a Finnish Nigerian journalist who has propagated information on African feminist issues, about the African diaspora, and Nigerian women through her award-winning blog MsAfropolitan, which she created and has been editing since 2010.

SHALINI SINHA is a lecturer in non-Western philosophy at the University of Reading. She received her PhD from the University of Sussex and has previously taught at the University of York and SOAS (University of London). Her research focuses on topics in Indian philosophy, primarily Hindu and Buddhist metaphysics and ethics, philosophy of mind and philosophy of action.

SIMONE WEBB is completing her PhD in Gender Studies at University College London. Her work puts Mary Astell into dialogue with the later ethical work of French thinker Michel Foucault, arguing that they can illuminate each other as well as providing useful guidance for modern feminist praxis. As well as academic interests in early modern philosophy, Foucauldian ethics and Pierre Hadot's *Philosophy as a Way of Life*, she is committed to public and community philosophy, regularly volunteering with the Stuart Low Trust philosophy forum. Her undergraduate degree was in Philosophy, Politics and Economics at the University of Oxford, and her master's in Women's Studies is from the same university.

LISA WHITING is a policy researcher in areas concerning practical ethics. She currently works for the Centre for Data Ethics and Innovation and is completing her master's degree in Government, Policy and Politics at Birkbeck, University of London, following her undergraduate degree in Philosophy at Durham University.

Unbound is the world's first crowdfunding publisher, established in 2011.

We believe that wonderful things can happen when you clear a path for people who share a passion. That's why we've built a platform that brings together readers and authors to crowd-fund books they believe in – and give fresh ideas that don't fit the traditional mould the chance they deserve.

This book is in your hands because readers made it possible. Everyone who pledged their support is listed below. Join them by visiting unbound.com and supporting a book today.

Nettie Abbott
Ricardo Abend
    van Dalen
Mac Acabado
Peter Adamson
Sam Affolter
Amber Agha
Karl Aho
Rufaida Al Hashmi
Diala Al Masri
Huda Alawaji
Tasha Alden
Tasha Alevropoulos-
    Borrill
Sandra K. Alexander
Alexis
Laura Allen

María Alonso
    Bustamante
Andrés Álvarez
Carolina Alves
Andreas Alving
Tina Ambury
Adam An-tAthair-Síoraí
James Andow
Jimmy Andrello
andykisaragi
Florence Angelo
Rani Lill Anjum
Christian Ankerstjerne
Steven Antalics
Alexandros
    Antonopoulos
Elias Anttila

Aisling Aquilina
Jacqueline Archibald
Craig Arko
Taline Artinian
Jessica Ash
Richard Ashcroft
Sarah Ashley
Lauren Ashwell
Tamsin Asquith
Devin Atkins
Elizabeth Axe
Júlia Ayerbe
James Aylett
Jen Ayling
Louise Bacharach
Sondra Bacharach
Sophie Bainbridge

Katy Balagopal
Holger Ballweg
Emily Bamford
Abineash Barathan
Rachel Barber
Natalia Bardini
Elisabeth Bargès
Mathew Barlow
Professor Ravinder Barn
Naomi Barnes
Teresa Baron
Sara Barratt
Colin Barrett
Andrew Bartel
Dr. Anke Bartels
Laura Bartolini
Ann-Sophie Barwich
Ben Basing
Michael D. Baumtrog
Hanna Bax
Jo Bayly
Emily Bayly Elsmore
Rosalind Bayly Elsmore
Emily Beatty
Ana Beaven
Jackson Beckner
Teresa Bejan
Emily Bell
Emma Bell
Saurabh Belsare
Michael Bench-Capon
David Bennett
M Bennett
Lisa Benson
Federica Berdini
Leda Berio
Flora Bernard
Ana Luisa Bernardino
Dominic Berry
Chris Bertram
Matea Beslic
Matthew Bess
Fauve Bickerstaffe
Helen Bilton
Jonathan Bindloss
Dr Tom D Binnie
Will Binzi

Jessica Bird
Laura Blair
Laia Blanc
Rose Blockeel
Holly Blood
Mark Blundell
Hannah Blythe
Henry Bolshaw
Becky Bolton
Lucy Bolton
Kim Bond
Jennifer Boon
Michelle Boon
Sarah Borwick
Ryan Bosley
Lucas Boulding
Michel Bourban
Jackie Bourke
David Boutland
Deborah Bowman
Ali Boyle
Claire Bracegirdle
Rebecca Bradfield
Seamus Bradley
Michael Brady
James Brandon
John Bridson
Liam Bright
Sarah Bright
Jacqueline Broad
Martin Brodetsky
Liz Bronder
Pascale Bronder
Andrew Brook
Gary Brooks
Matthew Broome
Lisa Broussois
Donna Brown
Jemma Brown
Paul Brown
Stuart Brown
Brian Browne
Stephen Bruce
Michael Bruckner
Jenny Bryan
Ollie Buckley
Joeri Buhrer Tavanier

Mia Buhrer Tavanier
Hung Bui
Katie Bullard
Jenny Bunker
Assia Buono
Peter Burnett
Frank Burr
Thea Burton
Daniel Butt
Matthew Butt
Richard Buxton
Simon Buxton
Alena Buyx
Daniel Callcut
Aifric Campbell
Ana Cannilla
Antonio Cantafio
Gerardo Capetillo
Maggie Capooci
Tom Carlson
Mary Carman
Rory Carroll-Maher
Brian A. Carter
Preston Carter
Alexandra Caruso
Mark Case Jr
Maude Casey
Lauren Cassani Davis
Jack Cassidy
Courtney Caton
Margarita Cavazos
Dirk Cavens
Axelle Cazeneuve
Lise Cazzoli
Celina
Joana Cerejo
Sarah Chaaban
Sarah Chadwick
Deborah Chalmers
David Chamberlain
Mary Chapin
Jane Charlesworth
Andy Charman
Cléo Chassonnery-
    Zaïgouche
Tom Chatfield
Ricardo Chavira

Darren Chetty
Amanda Chetwynd-
  Cowieson
Andrea Chlebikova
Phil Choi
Annie Cholewa
Lingying Chong
Jean Choo
Christina
Alice Chu
Steve Circeo
City of London School
  for Girls
Rachel Clack
Nick Clanchy
Carl Clare
Clare Clarke
Amina Clayton
Skye Cleary
Juliana Cliplef
Philippa Cochrane
Ann Cofell
Bethan Cole
Georgia Cole
Christopher Coles
Madeline Colin
Jennifer Collett Wright
Brian J. Collins
James Francis Collins
Kelly Colomberti
Sarah Colwell
Ruby and Teja Condliffe
Catherine Conneely
James Connelly
Orla Connolly
Hal Conyngham
Stephen Cook
Steve Cooke
Alison Coombs
Graihagh Cordwell
Erik Coronado
Andy Corsham
Simon Cottee
Josh Cottle
Michael Coughlin
Sam Couldrick
Anna Coundley

Lex Courts
Alexander Cox
Julia Cox
Robert Cox
Stephen Cox
Jessica Craig
Mary Crauderueff
Natalie Craw
Gabe Crisp
George Crosby
Harry Cross
Theo Crouch
Julia Croyden
Juliet Croydon
Richard Croydon
Ivan Croydon Veleslavov
Naomi Crudgington
Helen Crutcher
Kathrine Cuccuru
Felix Culas
Chris Cullen
David Curry
Maria Cygan
Michele D'Acosta
Benoit D'amours
Sarah Daley
James Dalton
F Dalzell
Elin Danielsen
  Huckerby
Davina Darmanin
Ben Davies
Richard Davies
Annalise Davis
Isaac Davis
Natalie Davis
Chloé de Canson
Nienke De Graeff
Manuel de Zubiría
Greg Dean
Philip William Deans
Alice Dee
Stephanie Deig
Megan Delehanty
Nathan DelMaramo
Alexander Delorme
Albert Delzeit

Manon Demulder
Katherine Devaney
Sophie Devlin
Ian Dickerson
Angela Dickson
Mary Dickson
Nancy Dickson
Dr Alix Dietzel
Alkistis Dimech
Amadea Paula Dodds
Joanna Dodds
Susan Dodds
Eric Dodson
Taylor Donahue
Arik Dondi
Linda Dong
Neelesh Dooraree
Dan Doran
Wendy Dossett
Alexander Douglas
Caroline Doveze
Matthew Downing
Logan Drake
Steve Drew
Manuel Driee
Frances Drinkall
Jo Drugan
Nicolas R. Dufour
James Duguid
Paul Dundon
Sarah Dunford
Jeremy Dunham
Gerry Dunne
Tabitha Dunthorne
Mike Dwyer
Jeanette Edge
David Edmonds
Josceline Edwards
Alia El-kholy
Alice el-Wakil
Eliza Elleston
Tae Ellin
Jasmine Elliott
Florian H. Elsishans
Patti Emerson
Andreas Emerson-
  Moering

Neele Engelmann
Gene Engene
Y J Erden
Johan Eriksson
Niklas Ernst
Phil Ertel
Emily Esch
Rob Estreitinho
Rob Evans
Thomas Everest-Dine
Joshua Everett
Jenneke Evers
Simon Evnine
Sara Ewad
Alex F
Nadira Faber
Joanne Farmer
Finbarr Farragher
Alessandra Fassio
Isabella Fausti
Feargus Fawsitt
Tracy Fells
Agata Ferretti
Juliette Ferry-Danini
Derek Fidler
Sarah Fine
Sarah Fisher
Robin Fisher Cisne
Warren Fitt
Jeff Flatt
William Fleming
Thaleia Flessa
Magen Flowers
Kevin B. Flowers, Jr.
Jane Flynn
Sarah Flynn
Jean Forbes
Robin Forrester
Anthoni Fortier
Camille Fouché
Sally Fowler
Frankie Fozard
Martine Frampton
Paul Freelend
Taylor French
Susan Frenk
Linda Fridh

Robert Friedrich
Ruwen Fritsche
Jerrie Froelich
Amie Fuentes
R Y Gaelic
James Gagen
Kezia Gaitskell
Anona Galbraith
Iain Galbraith
Diane Gall
Annemarie Gallagher
Esther Garcia Monreal
Anna & Shaun
Gardiner
Alan Garvey
Phil Gasper
Philip Gaydon
Marie-Emmanuelle
Genesse
Veleka Georgieva
Parastoo Geranmayeh
Sofie Gerits
Jean Gerster
Mollie Gerver
Rula Gianouchailidou
LaTonya Gibbs
Christopher-Marcus
Gibson
Matthew Gibson
Niamh Gibson
Richard Gidwaney
Kendall Gilfillan
Valentina Giusti
Christiane Glennie
GMarkC
Basia Godel
Stacey Goguen
Joey Goldman
Carlos Gomes
Moises Gonzalez
Horacio Gonzalez
Uresti
Brian Goodhart
Paul J Goodison
Bobby Goodson
Alison Gopnik
M Gordon

James Gorrie
Sam Gorse
Anthony Gorton
Jane Gould
Joanna Gower
Joe Grabiner
Alison Grace
Kathryn Grace
Ellen Grace Lesser
Anthony Graff
Will Graham
David Granberg
Eileen McKenzie Grant
Sophie Grant-Foale
Jake Gray
Esther Green
Sophie Green
Erin Greenough
Georgia Greer
Kallan Greybe
Sarah Grieves
Dani Griffin-Yates
Amber Griffioen
Simon Grönkvist
Eveline Groot
David Grover
Peter Grzic
Katy Guest
Jay A. Gupta
Louise Guthrie
Rebecca Gutwald
Ruby Guyatt
Dunya Habash
Joshua Habgood-Coote
Zerene Haddad
Andrew Hahm
Thomas Hainscho
Sue Haldemann
Cris Hale
Alan Hall
Niklas Hallin
Ina Hallström
Alexandra Halstead
Kathryn Elizabeth
Hamm
Ralph Hammond
Chris Hancock

Rachel Handley
Greg Hanscomb
Mollie Hantman-Weill
Aruna Manohar Haque
Siba Harb
Mahi Hardalupas
Sara Hardman
Alison Hardy
Kate Harford
Kristin Harnoth
Peter Harrigan
Ralph Harrington
Leann Harris
Nicky Harris
Jazz Harrison
Nova Hartanty
Bob Hartley
Mandy Hathaway
Katie Havelaar Cook
Kaleem Hawa
Katherine Hawes
Genevieve Hayman
Will Heaps
Emma Heasman-Hunt
Ben Heath
Andrew Hedley
Tuomas Heikkila
Sarah Hellawell
Daniel Hemings
Courtney Hempton
Robert Henderson
Christina Hendricks
Céline Henne
Caroline Hensman
Lucy Henzell-Thomas
Jean-François Héon
Kevin Hermberg
Emily Herring
Mark Herwicz
Thomas Hescott
Daisy Hesnan
Harry Hewitt
Tristan Heydolph
Heather Hicks
Gemma Hill
Giles Hill
Ahmed Hazyl Hilmy

Mike Hines
Karen Hinojosa
Sarah Hjorth Andersen
Megan Hoak
Angie Hobbs
Hannah Hobson
Michael Hocken
Emily Hodder
Rachel Hoekendijk
Camilla Ulleland Hoel
Gabriella Hoff
Matthew A. Hoffman
A.G. Holdier
Tobias Höller
Jordan Holmes
Molly Holmes
James Holroyd
Billy Holt
Stephanie Holton
Antonia Honeywell
Joel Hooper
Andrew Horton
Grace Horton
Jo Howard
David Howe
Caroline Huckvale
Stephen Hudson
Jonathan Hughes
Mark Hughes
Marnie Hughes-
  Warrington
Bernard Huguelet
Elisabeth Huh
Joanna Humphreys
Rosie Hunnam
Lucy Hunt
David Hunter
Sarah Hunter
Samia Hurst-Majno
Ibtehal Hussain
Leisha Hussien
Charlotte Hutchinson
Jade Huynh
Gareth Hynes
Yanitsa Ilieva
In Parenthesis
IngeniousPrairieDog

The Iris Murdoch
  Society
Victoria Isett
Julietta Ivanova
JD Ivey
Dr Sarah Birrell Ivory
Andrew Jackson
Ollie Jackson
Anne Jacobson
Hunter Jacobson
Thomas Jacques-
  Butterworth
Ravin Jain
Clare James
Emily James
Mike James
Willa James
Eric Janec
Andrew Janiak
Zoe Jardiniere
Billy Jarvis
James Jefferies
Christian Jeffery
Becca Jiggens
Noelia Jiménez
  Martínez
Adam Jobling
Christopher Johnson
Robert Johnson
Susannah Johnson
Carla Johnston
Emily Jones
Jacob Jones
Julie Jones
Andreas Jonson
Kim Jordan
Lindsay Jordan
Patrick W. Jordan
Zoe Jordan
Max Kaehn
Lena Kainz
Christina
  Kalogeropoulou
Tomislav Karačić
Alessa Maria Karešin
Sukbir Kaur
Amy Kean

Joan Keating
Leslie Keating
Marcella Keating
Jan Keeling
Andrej Kelemen
Mike Kelley
Hannah Kelly
Adam Kennedy
K Kennedy
Kathryn Kenny
Oliver Kenny
Jenny Kermally
Dan Kieran
Jill Kieran
Meg Kilmister
Laura Kilty
Maureen Kincaid
  Speller
Katharine King
Rebekah King
Sally King
Lara Kirfel
Matt Kirk
Matthew Kirk
Joseph Kisolo-Ssonko
Julie Klein
Ryan Klein
Rafal Klosek
Benjamin Knutson
Harleen Kochar
Catherine Koekoek
Verena Kogelbauer
Joanne Louise Kohler-
  Groves
Bibi Kok
Avery Kolers
Varuna Kollanethu
Cornelia Korinth
Ernestine Kossmann
Gabriella Kountourides
Teresa Kouri Kissel
Wilson Kozlowski
Lili Kramer
Gary Krenz
Jenny Krutzinna
Jacek Kruza
Joachim Kübler

Ulrike Kuchner
Karin Kuhlemann
Vijay Kumar
Theophilus Kwek
Andy Lacroce
Melinda Laituri
Ryan Lake
lalalalilly
Dianne Lalonde
Susan Lamb
David Lambert
Georgina Lambert
Felix Lambrecht
Rafael Lameiro da
  Costa Rocha
Miriam Lander
Nicole Landers
Lynn Landry
Karen Langley
Christopher Lanyon
George Lanyon
Holly Lanyon
Lee Large
Mark Larson
Dr Jenny Louise
  Lawrence
Freya Marie Lawton
Ruth Le Ber
Jimmy Leach
Catherine Leach-
  Phillips
Amy Leask
Diana Lee
Elizabeth Lee
Simon Angseop Lee
Phillip Lemky
Martin Lenz
Eréndira León
Daniel Leufer
Paul Levy
Anastasia Lewis
Deborah Lewis
Dwight Lewis
Richard Lewis
Yin-Hsuan Liang
Azzurra Liberatori
Winnie Lim

Peter Jesse Linton
Robert Lister
Clayton Littlejohn
Dawn Llewellyn
Hilary Lloyd
Vikki Lloyd
Dean Lo Seen Chong
Christopher Lockyear
Mikkel Lodahl
Paul Lodge
Shane Lohnes
Sarah Londo
The London Public
  Philosophy Club
Amie-Rose Long
Heather Longworth
William Longworth
Veronika Lönner
Vincent Lostanlen
Abi Lovell
Lulita Lu Hui
Jeanita Lyman
Vera Rolfine Fryd
  Lyngmo
Aaron Luisa Lyons
Ben Lyons
Georgia Lyttle
Maya Lyttle
Melusine Ma
Amy Mabey
Laura MacArthur
Chris MacDonald
Karen Mace
Lindsay Macgregor
Jon Mackenzie
Conor Mackey
Malcolm MacLean
Iain Macniven
Edith MacQuarrie
Jonathan Madeland
Oran Magal
Victor Magnusson
Emma Major
Catherine Makin
Carol Malleson
Rose Malleson
Gustaf Malmberg

Aaron Maniam
Stephen Francis Mann
Lynn Mari
Paloma Marín Ortiz
Gustavo Mariscal
  Guinea
Angela Marjoram
Katie Marjoram
Xander Marjoram
Mark
Deborah Markham
Lucie Marley
Oliver Marley
Niamh Marren
Eugene Marshall
Lisa Marti
Philip Martin
Adrián Martínez
Jorge Martínez Ortega
Florian Marwede
Viktoria Matejova
Samuel Mather
Rebecca McBain
Lauren McCarthy
Rebecca McCarthy
Andrew McCulloch
James McDaniel
Meghan McDermott
Matthew McDougall
Gregory McElwain
Lorna McGhee
Marie McGinley
Aidan McGlynn
Declan McGrath
Tina McGrath PhD
Rebecca McGuckin
Hannah McIntyre
Sam McKavanagh
Felicity McKay
David McKenna
Rosie McKenna
Tamsyn McLean
April McNeely
Dr Lisa Mcnulty
Aidan McQuade
Marina Meffert
MegElizabethABC

Trevor Meier
Christian Meinke
Stephen Meister
Peter Meldrum
Torsten Menge
Sina Menke
Luke Menniss
Rebecca Metzer
Derek A. Michaud
Nicole Milkereit
Gregory Miller
Laura Miller on behalf
  of Eton College
Millie
Mercedes Milligan
Richard Milton
Michelle Mirick
Eamonn Mitchell
Lesley Mitchell
John Mitchinson
Robert Mittendorf
Corey Mohler
Roland Möller
William Molloy
Katherine Montalto
Krista Montgomery
James Moore
Rebecca Moore
Azucena Moran
Lisa Moresco
Anthony Morgan
Julie Moronuki
Bev Morris
David Morrow
Kelsie Morton
Katrina Moseley
Peter Moskalew
Giulietta Mottini
Romeu Moura
Nathalie Moyaert
Vanina Mozziconacci
Laura Muchmore
Joerg Mueller-Kindt
Deborah Mühlebach
Nikhil Mulani
Michael Mullan-Jensen
Rebecca Mullen

Joachim Müller
Rachel Mullin
Ailsa Mullins
Judy Munday
Julia Muñoz
Christian Munthe
Callum Murray
Venkatesh Murthy
Stephen Musgrave
Linda Mutunga
Madhuram Nagarajan
Michael Nagenborg
Will Nalls
Tatiana Nardi
Deborah Nash
Shelley Nation
Carlo Navato
David and Christine
  Naylor
Rémy Naylor
Antony Nelson
Margaret Nelson
Suzanna Nelson-Pollard
Julia Netter
Alexandra Neufeld
Jared Neumann
Emma Neviile
Tilly Nevin
Rebecca Newberger
  Goldstein
Oliver Newton
Sian Ng
Annalisa Nicholson
Josef Nickerson
Sue Nieland
Lasse Nielsen
Magnus Nilsson
Michael Nitabach
Christopher Nixon
Judi Noakes
Melissa Nolas
Tasha Nussbaum
Emma Nygård
Lisa O'Connor
Damian O'Dea
Jenny O'Gorman
Warren O'Keefe

Shona O'Keeffe
Kathleen O'Neal
Sally O'Neill
Katharine O'Reilly
Ciara O'Sullivan
Georgia Odd
Bonne Odiorne
Emily Rose Ogland
Clara Ohayon
Sue Oldfield
Vernie Oliveiro
Dani Oliver
Gregory Olver
Ashley Orr
Susan Orr
Fernanda Ortega
Monica Osorio
  Malfitano
Aaron Ostler
Lucy Oulton
Miranda Owen
  Wintersgill
Sinan Özyürek
Rachel Paine
Sharad Pandian
Jun Pang
Ourania
  Papasozomenou
Dillon Euell Pape
Nick Parfitt
Robert Park
Colleen Parker Bacquet
John Parry
T.C. Partridge
Dean Paton
Liv Pattison
Thomas Paulmichl
Sonia Maria Pavel
Fergus Peace
Gareth R Pearce
Simon John Pearce
Trevor Pearce
Sabrina Peck
Jacques Pelletier
A.J. Perger
Ron Perkins
Morgan Petersen

Charlie Peterson
Jennifer Peterson
Gunnel Pettersson
Kirstin Pettet
Richard Pettigrew
Quentin Pharr
Kristopher Phillips
Philosophy Tube
Matt Pierri
Megan Pike
Heidi Pio
Adeline Pival
J Platzky Miller
Jana Pleger-Martin de la
  Hinojosa de la Puerta
Edwin Ploye
Rachel Plummer
Justin Pollard
Lauren Polzin
Neil Polzin
Danielle Pomeroy
Iona Popat
Eva-Maria Popp
Eric Porter
Samantha Potter
Karen Powell
Chris Power
Amy Preston-Samson
Lillian Primrose
Sebastien Provencher
Malwina Przyborowska
Charlotte Pyle
Anna Quinn
Emma Quinn
Katharine Quinn
Eve Rabinoff
Lucia M. Rafanelli
Esme Rajecki-Doyle
Lee Rambo
Urszula Rapacka
Katherine Rasmussen
Seyed Razavi
Colette Reap
Jalees Reehman
Stephanie Regalia
Rob Reich
Julie Reid

Simon Reigh
Gijs Reudink
Mack and Rachel Lee
  Reynolds
Una Richmond
Gregory Riggs
Shannon W Rigney
Afra Rijkhoff
Liam Riley
Euan Ritchie
Sam Ritholtz
Scott B. Ritner
RMR
Amy Roberts
Kathryn Roberts
JG Robertson
Jess Robins
Christine Robinson
Sarah Robinson
Brenda N. Rodriguez
Robert Houston
  Rodriguez
Latika Rodway-Anand
Timothy Roes
Bernard & Maria Ropp
Robyn Roscoe
Melanie Rosenthal
Brooke Rudow
Greg Rupik
Michael Rush
Gillian Russell
Karina Russell
Helena Rutkowska
Miquel Sabaté
Josephine Salverda
Valentin Sanchez
Clara Sandelind
Vanessa Sanders
Iván Sandoval-Cervantes
Beatriz Santos
Caitlin Saunders
Shrikant Sawant
Carol Sayles
John Scarr
Matthieu Schaller
Stefan Schindler
Nicole Schippel

Birgit Schmidt
Christina Schmidt
Tommy Schmucker
Tim Scott
Johan Seidenfaden
Anna Sekuła
Amit Sen
Kara-Jane Senior
Thomas Senor
Kieran Setiya
David Severson
Zachary Shank
Lisa Shapiro
Danial Shariat
Francesca Sharman
Rachael Shaw
Sarah Shepherd
Hannah Sheppard
Phil Sheppard
Carrie & Steven Sheret
Brooke Sheridan
Dorothy Shinn
Michael Shockley
Bolonie Shuhaibar
Matt Silec
Mary Silva
Elizabeth Silvolli
Joshua Simmons
Luma Simms
Daniel Simon
Deanna Simpson
Emily Simpson
Sammy Sinno
Aik Siong
Maks Sipowicz
Rob Sips
Jennifer Sizer
William Sked
Raven Skobe
Adam Skoglund
Joe Slater
Lauren Slater
Zora Slavik
Gabriela Smarrelli
Kai Smart
Aaron Smith
Alice Smith

Emmy Smith
Katie Smith
Sharon Smith
Stephen Smith
Yel Smith
J Smits
Grace Sneesby
Donna Snyder
Anthony Solomonides
Timothy Southon
Alice Sowaal
Kerri J Spangaro
Amanda Sparshott
Carrie Spencer
Frank W Spencer
Lucienne Spencer
Saige James Spjut
David Spurrett
St. John's College MCR,
    Oxford
John Stafford
Freya Stanley-Price
Esje Stapleton
Mog Stapleton
Gina Starfield
Susan Stead
Anne Marie Steiger
Britta Stein
Joshua Stein
Janet Stemwedel
Marilyn Stendera
Adam Stephens
Natalia Sterling
Jana Stern
David Stevens
Iona Stevenson
Elizabeth Stewart
Daniel Stock
Amy Stockdale
Carter Stoddard
Susanne Stolz
Theodore Stone
Allison Strachan
Juan Strisino
Emily & Rebecca
    Strong
Susan Stuart

Ander Suárez
Timo Sulg
James Sullivan
Ema Sullivan-Bissett
Christopher Sunami
Moe Suzuki
Sigrún Sveinsdóttir
Adam Swallow
Hunter Swenson
    HunterSwen
Deb Swinney
Jack Symes
Nora Tabel
Tisse Takagi
Rosa Tallack
Cathrine Talleraas
Zailyn Tamayo
Tony Tambasco
Millie Tanner
Alex Tarrant-Anderson
Helen Taylor
Nicola Taylor
Scott Taylor
Laura Taylor Innes
Alison Tazelaar
Chon Tejedor
Cassandra Telenko
Hadnet Tesfom
Mélanie Thienard
Alison Thimmesch
George Thomas
Pierrette Thomet
Rachel Thompson
Kenneth Thomson-
    Duncan
Pip Thornley
Erin Rose Myfanwy
    Thornton
Frida Tiberini
Laura Tidd
John J. Tilley
Sheila Tindal
Louise Tizzard
Yevgeniya Tomkiv
Jenny Tomlinson
Mia Tong Atasever
Clotilde Torregrossa

Alberto Torres
Mª Teresa Torres Valderrama
Frida Trotter
Kelly Truelove
Voula Tsoflias
Emma Tumilty
Hugh Turner
Sarah Turner
Richard Tweedie
Bindu Upadhyay
Robert Upton
TJ Usiyan
Tere Vaden
Clair Vainola
Alexyz Valdes
Rens van Bergeijk
Berend van der Kolk
Johannes van der Vos
Aart van Gils
John van Kooy
Carolien van Welij
Tony Vanderheyden
Janet Vaughan
Johnnie Vaughn
Juan Vazquez
Walter Veit
Gregory Velazco y Trianosky
Aurora Venancio
Nikhil Venkatesh
Elizabeth Ventham
Verdandi
Camila Vergara
Knut Jørgen Vie
Alejandro Villalobos
Sander Vink
Alnica Visser
Diana Vladutu
Maya von und zur Mühlen
Joe Wadsworth
Karla Waegeman
Elizabeth Wakeman
Victoria Walden
Allison Walker
Bradley Wallace

Anna Wallin
Jacqueline Mae Wallis
Eve Walmsley
Michael Walschots
Patrick F. Walsh
Karen Walton
Nigel Warburton
Simon Ward
Taryn Ward
Amy Ware
Lauren Ware
Ruth Wareham
Emily Warnakulasuriya
Ruth Waterton
Ashley Watson
Bryony Watson
Jordan Watson
Laura Watson
Lynelle Watts
Gareth Webb
Elizabeth Webster
Julia Wei
Brian Weis
Simon Weisenbach
Dr. Sabrina M. Weiss
Amila Welihinda
A Welsby
Mike Wernecke
Andy West
Anne Wheeldon
Anaïs Rebecca White
Mark D. White
Cecily Whiteley
Ali Whiting
Charyl and Graham Whiting
Veerle Wijffels
Julia Wilam
Rob Wilkinson
Jenny Williams
Myfanwy Williams
Phil Williams
Rachel Williams
Steven Ivan Williams
Tina Williams
Pamela Williamson
Julia Willich

Alice Wilson
Dawn Wilson
Joan Wilson
Amy Winchester
Josh Windmiller
J. Wing
Jos Wingfield
Robyn Winklareth
Yasmin Winslade
Jake Wojtowicz
Jonathan Wolff
David Wolkensperg
Naomi Woo
Caitlin Wood
Christopher Woodard
James Woodbridge
Annabelle Woodger
Jody Woodland
Bryony Woods
Pamela Woods
Simon Woods
Garrett Woodward
Oli Woolley
Clemency Woolner
Emma Worley
John Worne
Laura Wreschnig
Charlotte Wright
Louise Wu
Stephanie Wykstra
Wayne Wylupski
Natasha Wynne
Greg Yerkes
Crystal Young
Damon Young
Debbie Young
Rachel L. Yzelman
Richard Zach
K Melissa Zahradnicek
Robin Zebrowski
Lia Zehnder
Tiger Zheng
Magnus Møller Ziegler
Costantina G. Zorpa
Jacob Zuiderveen